May You Live in Christ!

Spiritual Growth Through The Vision of St. Peter

Robert T. Jennings

Copyright 2014 Robert T. Jennings.
All rights reserved.
ISBN: 1499182341
ISBN 13: 9781499182347

The Scripture quotations contained herein are from the New Revised Standard Version Bible, copyright, 1989, by the Division of Christian Education of the National Council of the Churches of Christ in the U.S.A. Used by permission. All rights reserved.

Cover: The Statue of St. Peter. c. 1838-1840 (marble) sculpted by Giuseppe De Fabris (1790-1860). St. Peter's Basilica, Vatican City. iStockphoto

Cover Design: Michelle Knox, Lone Red Design, LLC

To our sons,
Ben, Rob, John, and David
for their character, sacrifice,
honor, and love
and for their life in Christ

Contents

Acknowledgements..........vii

Introduction The Vision: May you live in Christ!..........xi

Part One   **Receiving the Vision**
    1   Everything
         Burnand, *Peter and John Running to the Tomb*..........2

    2   Glory
         Raphael, *The Transfiguration of Christ*..........12

    3   Faith
         Delacroix, *St. Peter Walking on the Water*..........25

Part Two   **Seeing the Vision**
    4   Goodness
         James, *Feeding the Five Thousand*..........36

    5   Knowledge
         Duccio, *The Calling of the Apostles Peter and Andrew*..........48

    6   Self-Control
         Rembrandt, *Peter Denouncing Christ*..........59

    7   Endurance
         Wesley, *Jesus Healing the Leper*..........71

Part Three **Living the Vision**
    8   Godliness
         Ethiopian Icon, *Jesus Washing Peter's Feet*..........84

    9   Mutual Affection
         Tabgha, Israel, *The Statue of Jesus and Peter*..........95

    10   Love
         Caravaggio, *Crucifixion of St. Peter* 107

11 Benediction
Grow in Grace and Knowledge
The Vatican, *The Statue of St. Peter*..........119

Image Credits..........123

Acknowledgements

A book like this is never written in solitude. Of course, I am sitting alone in the silence as I write. I am surrounded, however, by hundreds of thoughts and experiences and people—most of all people. They are people of all walks and stripes who have entered my life and who still surround me as a "great cloud of witnesses."

The people of St. Francis in the Fields, Harrods Creek, Kentucky, in particular helped me over thirty years of ministry write this book. They listened to me when I said the same thing over and over again. They probably could finish my sentences. More importantly, they showed up. They were there in church worshipping the living God Sunday in and Sunday out. I see them in their pews. They sat in the same places. I missed them when they were not there. I enjoyed their presence. They were there for baptisms and weddings and funerals. Through the weeks, I often thought I was ministering to them. The reality was, of course, they were ministering to me. It was in this mutual care for one another we prayed and we shared our concerns and above all we witnessed to our faith. It is to this faith community I am indebted. It was here—in church—I began to see and have a vision for spiritual growth in Jesus Christ.

I preached this message. I also taught it to a group on Tuesday mornings. It was Bible study. It was more than that. Over the years, it became apparent to all that as we were pouring over the sacred texts, we "saw with our eyes and we touched with our hands the word of life" (I John 1:1). We were slow learners. But we did learn. As a group, it became apparent we were not the ones who were studying the Bible. No, the Bible was studying us. And the "word became flesh and dwelt among us" (John 1:14). It was that simple. It was also that profound. I will always be indebted to this group for witnessing to this powerful transformation of our life in Christ.

A book like this is never written in solitude. Swirling around me are all these warm memories. There are also people who brought me back to earth. I could not have written this book without the steady hand and guidance of Jill and Doug Keeney. Together, they formed an editorial team that helped me think through what I was trying to say, and with their professional eye, they helped me to see the process of publishing from beginning to end. I am indebted to Ralinda Gregor as well, who laboriously and patiently proofread every word and made this book come alive. There are countless others. Jeff Skinner sat with me early on and talked with me about the art of writing a book and the need for a framework and a spinal cord from which everything hangs. Alex Campbell joined me in a steady, thoughtful conversation as we read and discussed the book, along with Mac Shwab and the Wednesday-night study group. I received from them the encouragement to write the study questions at the end of each chapter. This book would never have seen the light of day without Melodie Fridley. She was the one who revised and typeset page after page again and again and again. Finally, I want to thank the V. V. Cooke Foundation for catching hold of this proposal and helping with the burden of much of the initial expense.

As with any writer who is married and who has children and now grandchildren, there is another life. A book can take on a life of its own. My wife, Mary, showed me where life is really lived, and with her insight and vision, she provided me with a balance and an understanding of love that "bears all things and believes all things" (I Corinthians 13:7). She gave me as well the gift of our four sons, to whom this book is dedicated.

Rev. Robert T. Jennings

2 Peter 1:3-7

His divine power has given us everything needed for life and godliness, through the knowledge of him who called us by his own glory and goodness. Thus he has given us, through these things, his precious and very great promises, so that through them you may escape from the corruption that is in the world because of lust, and may become participants of the divine nature. For this very reason, you must make every effort to *add to* your faith with goodness, and goodness with knowledge, and knowledge with self-control, and self-control with endurance, and endurance with godliness, and godliness with mutual affection, and mutual affection with love.

Throughout our study, we will use the imperative of the Greek "to add" to our faith. This translation more closely resembles St. Peter's understanding that God is the generous giver who contributes or adds to our faith through the divine nature of Jesus Christ.

See *The Message of 2 Peter & Jude*, by Dick Lucas and Christopher Green (Downers Grove, IL, InterVarsity Press, 1995) p. 57.

May You Live in Christ!

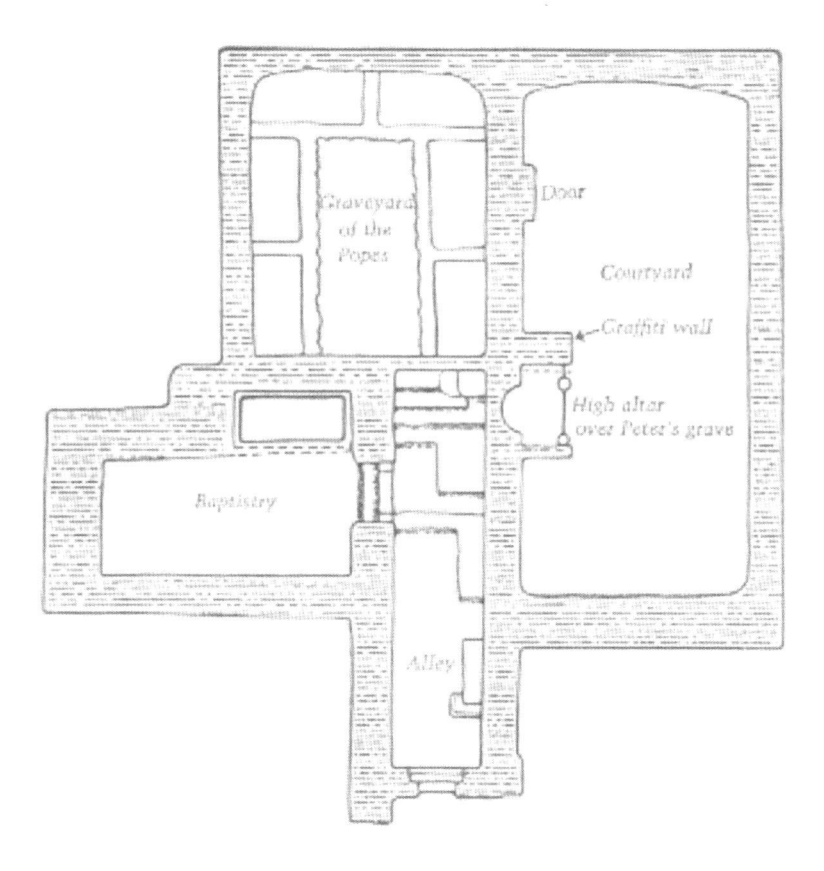

[Floor plan diagram with labels: Graveyard of the Popes, Door, Courtyard, Graffiti wall, High altar over Peter's grave, Baptistery, Alley]

The ancient floor plan above suggests what the excavation in 1939 under the Vatican might have revealed. A red wall surrounding a courtyard could have held as many as 75 first-century Christians who gathered for worship. The focal point was Peter's grave. Over the grave was an altar to celebrate life in Christ revealed through the Eucharist. The altar covered the grave from looting but Peter's presence was known.

The close proximity of the graveyard and the baptistery, along with the inscription on the wall – *Vivatis in Christo!* May you live in Christ! – cast the vision of participating in the divine nature for all who worshipped.

From: *The Bones of St. Peter: The first full account of the search for the Apostle's body.* John Evangelist Walsh. Sophia Institute Press. 1982.

Introduction

May You Live in Christ

Under the Vatican, hidden far below the high altar of St. Peter's Basilica in Rome, one of the most sacred spots in all of Christendom can be found. Although it is removed from the lines of most tourists where cameras are strictly forbidden, in the dark, claustrophobic setting of this sacred space, a few visitors each day are permitted a quiet moment to gaze, reflect, and pray near the bones of St. Peter.

For some believers, relics are revered because they hold power and energy in their own right. What makes this spot different and holy is here, in the quiet and natural setting of death—standing in the presence of St. Peter—a vision for life is given.

The story of this vision came to light in 1939. At this time, it was determined that extensive alterations were needed on the basement floor level of the Basilica for additional papal burial sites and for the safety of not only the crypts but also the actual foundation of the church structure.

Since the Vatican at the time would not permit the use of power tools, work underneath this massive historical and religious site was painstakingly and methodically slow. Carefully, workers equipped with only shovels and trowels and wheelbarrows and limited lighting began to scrape and dig their way under the floor.

As the digging progressed, the small group of workmen—much to their surprise—found the underlying soil giving way and opening up a large hole, which revealed a cavern of considerable space well below the massive church building.

It was like something out of *Indiana Jones*. Reports of the discovery traveled all the way up to the pope himself, and the original construction project was now transformed into an entirely new archeological study. As some 6,000 cubic feet of dirt were removed from down below, ancient city walls and a main road dating back to the first and second centuries were discovered. In addition, a strange collection of burial tombs was found. Unlike the early underground catacombs throughout historic Rome, these burial spots were positioned in a unique formation. The bodies had been laid to rest in a circle with the heads all facing a mound at the center.

Christian inscriptions and Christian symbols and early Christian art surrounded the wall of this apparent graveyard. Dating back to 150 AD, one inscription read "Peter, pray Christ Jesus for the holy…" (cf. I Peter 1:16), only to end there, the remaining words in the sentence obliterated by time and erosion.

As scholars began to wrestle with their findings, their work seemed far removed from the events of World War II. Yet it was now probable that what was being uncovered in the darkness below the Vatican was the very tomb of St. Peter. Perhaps this grave could somehow bring light to a world ravaged by darkness and the war above.

The Discovery

As one discovery gave way to another, a brick with Christian graffiti was found near the mound with the inscription *"Vivatis in Christo!"* which, translated, means "May you live in Christ!" More than words, what appeared here was a liturgical benediction, or a baptismal expression, or a Eucharistic blessing. Scholars suggest this blessing could well have been articulated by St. Peter and spoken to his faithful and said as a liturgical expression within the context of worship. So it was here, near the wall and under the mound, archeologists uncovered the grave and the bones of St. Peter. The bodies of those encircled around the mound were identified as early popes who wanted their heads or minds buried close to the mind of St. Peter, whose mind and whose life were in Christ—forever.

The discovery not only revealed the burial spot of Peter's bones but what was made public after years of excavation and centuries of being hidden was a holy space, a sacred underground place, where first-century Christians gathered for worship and celebrated the breaking of the bread of life and the rite of baptism into the kingdom of this new life with God.

The understanding was clear and simple: life is available in Jesus. "The life that really is life" (I Timothy 6:19) is life in Christ. It is life-with-God, meaning it is life eternal—it is life forever. From this primitive first-century worship space located directly beneath the altar of St. Peter's that towered above, early Christians greeted one another and formed a faith community around a clear and simple vision: *Vivatis in Christo!* May you live in Christ! This book is designed to help us see that what was a vision then can continue as we participate in the divine nature of Christ today.

Growth Points

With this vision comes growth in Christ. In our growth in Christ, we experience life eternal—a life that is abundant—life that is with God. We discover as well points of growth that reflect a change from the way we have lived and from the way we have been. Growth points keep us on track. Growth points expand our vision, open our eyes, and help us see God at work in our lives like never before. Christian life, vision, and growth are all first and foremost spiritual. I remember when our boys were young and my wife would measure their physical heights with a measuring tape and by making marks inside a kitchen door. The sight of them growing from year to year or, in some cases, from month to month was always a cause of great excitement.

Measuring growth in the spiritual life is, of course, harder. Unlike all other aspects of our lives, the spirit resides at the innermost part of our being and it is not visible to the eye. The fact that we do not see something, however, does not mean it does not exist. The writer of Hebrews says, "Now faith is the assurance of things hoped for, the conviction of things not seen" (11:1). Faith imparts vision.

Faith also measures growth. As we will see, faith will provide us with a spiritual vision that is less about eyesight and more about insight. The things not seen are spiritual things. Faith will mark our spiritual growth and our conviction not with a measuring tape in inches and feet but by identifying points of growth as we mature and develop in our life in Christ. Each chapter will open with a point of growth that will help us describe how God is at work in our lives. At the close of each chapter, we will identify a stepping stone that will direct us toward the growth point. Each chapter will be organized as follows:

- Art will help picture the vision for our life in Christ;
- A growth point embedded in 2 Peter will focus our vision;
- Spiritual growth begins with life in Christ; and
- A stepping stone from Peter will help us get started.

The Vision for Our Life in Christ

Here is an example: Remember the map that opened this chapter? We used it to help us reflect on the discovery of the early Christians' vision: *Vivatis in Christo!* May you live in Christ! Now let's use the map like a painting to help us picture the vision for our life in Christ. By starting with the map and the discovery of the words "May *you* live in Christ," we are aware that this vision is personal. It speaks to *you*. May *you* live in Christ. Living in Christ is up close and personal. This vision is designed to move *you*, personally.

Now, to make this vision even more personal, it says, "May you live *in* Christ." The little preposition "in" is enormous. I could say I believe *that* Christ was a great man. I could say that I stand *by* Christ. It would be easy to say I am *with* Christ or I am *on* the side of Christ. But what does it mean to say I live *in* Christ? It means my faith in Christ is not propositional but it is very personal. It means that by living in Christ my life is interrelated and interacting and interconnected with his life just as he is interrelated and interacting and interconnected with my life. To be in Christ, then, speaks of a conversion or a transformation so that my character is now formed and shaped in his character. Such character formation in Christ is immortal and eternal.

Growth Point—Life

The early Christians faced persecution and death. Life in Christ was important because, obviously, it beat death. To be sure, this understanding of life in Christ was helpful after they died. But St. Peter experienced life in Christ as a life that is eternal and is activated here on earth—now. As a result, believers did not need to physically die before life in Christ could be fully discovered and participated in right then—in this present existence—and within the immediate demands of everyday, ordinary life.

The Greeks had two words for life. One word to describe life was *bios*. It is a way of thinking about our mortal life or our biological life. In many respects, this life is physically limited. Along with this physical mortality, the Greeks also thought of an immortal life that could be described through the word *zoe*. Zoe life was a life that was never ending. The Gospel of John, as an example, was written in the Greek language, and John records it like this: "What has come into being in him was life (zoe), and the life (zoe) was the light of all people." (John 1:3)

"May you live in Christ" speaks to the faithful about this zoe life and this different vision for living. In Christ, we live and move and have our being right now with God—forever. In addition, life in Christ opens us to life in his Kingdom, where we come under his rule and his governance. Trusting in Christ as Lord of our lives is found not when we die but is made available to us, at this very moment, as we live through the power of the resurrection of Jesus. Life in Christ is therefore a resurrected life that breaks through the boundaries and limits of time, space, and memory so that we are free to participate in his divine nature.

Life in Christ

We are much like cats with nine lives. We have emotional lives, financial lives, family lives, political lives, work lives, and so on and so forth. We live many, many lives. Rather than living a life that is fractured, we try to take charge and control these many lives. Unfortunately, when we try to govern and rule all these lives, they are in turn measured and evaluated by our self-imposed guidelines, definitions, and criteria. The result is we soon live not only very broken lives but very self-centered lives.

Living in Christ presents a radically different vision from a broken, self-centered pursuit. So too does growing in Christ. When we live and grow in Christ, we change in Christ. Growth and change often accompany one another. As we place our trust and confidence in Jesus as Lord of our lives, we change and we live centered lives by growing in Christ. By living into centered lives in Christ, we then integrate all of our many lives into one life—the Christian life. It is again here in Christ we begin to interrelate and interact and interconnect with him. We talk with him. Yes, we walk with him. We listen to his words. We do what Christ says. Ultimately, our character is formed and shaped and we begin to do what comes naturally to our life in Christ. Our human nature becomes transformed and converted by this spiritual nature. We are born again. Or, as St. Paul writes, "It is no longer I who live but Christ who lives in me…" (Galatians 2:20). Conversion in Christ changes and transforms the way we live.

One example of this changed life is found in the life of St. Peter. Peter was by no means perfect. He made mistakes. Recall the haunting words of Jesus to Peter: "The spirit is willing, but the flesh is weak" (Matthew 26:41). Growth begins often at our weakest point. Here the seed of God's amazing grace is planted and growth occurs. The life in Christ allows us to do those things we have been unable to do on our own.

The Double Helix: Grace and Knowledge

At the end of St. Peter's second letter to the church are these words: "But grow in the grace and knowledge of our Lord and Savior Jesus Christ" (2 Peter 3:18).

The vision of St. Peter is strengthened by this double helix of grace and knowledge. Grace comes when we know Christ is helping us grow. Knowledge of growth in Christ comes from his grace. The two—grace and knowledge—work together, revealing our life and our spiritual growth in Christ. St. Peter will show us how this double helix—this lifegiving spiritual cell of grace and knowledge—works in forming and shaping not only our souls but our very destinies. Grace and knowledge in Christ begins for St. Peter with his mishaps, mistakes, and weaknesses. These are the beginning of growth points.

These growth points are not just confined to one man. Peter represents everyman. Peter represents the church. When Peter doesn't get it, that is a gentle reminder that there are days when we don't get it. But that is not all. What reverberates deep within Peter's soul is that, in the darkest hour, he discovers the light and the vision and the blessings and the life eternal and the grace and the knowledge that is now made holy in Christ.

Theologian Rudolf Otto called this holy life *mysterium tremendum et fascinans,* the mystery that both terrifies and fascinates. A vision has a way of doing just that—it terrifies and fascinates—but in Christ, we discover a vision for life that is holy. No one wants to be weak. We all want to be made strong. No one wants to be in the dark. We all want to be enlightened. Although most people are reluctant to change, most of us want to grow. Peter will be our guide and direct us by example through weakness and strength, darkness and light, change and growth, grace and knowledge on into the vision that awaits us in our life in Christ. Through the eyes of St. Peter, we will see what spiritual growth looks like, and from his experience, we will be given a vision of holiness to live our lives through our participation in the divine nature of Jesus Christ.

The Stepping Stone—Follow Me

Recall that Peter was by trade a fisherman. In fact, following the Crucifixion, he told his friends "I am going fishing" (John 21:3). Some would call this an act of apostasy, or a denial of faith. Another way of looking at it is that Peter needed some time—some space—to try to figure out what just happened during those dreadful few days in Jerusalem. His life was out of control. He was also terrified.

And so it was, just after daybreak as the Gospel story goes, while Peter was fishing, the resurrected Jesus stood on the beach and he called out to the disciples, "Children, you have no fish, have you?" Peter heard it was the Lord who was calling the disciples, and upon hearing the voice of Jesus, he dove into the sea and swam to the beach. There, Peter broke bread with the risen Lord and was in communion with Christ as the eternal life in Christ entered the life of Peter, who was growing both in grace and knowledge. The stepping stone was set as Jesus said to Peter, "Follow me."

"Follow me" is our stepping stone. In the chapters before us, we will follow Jesus and Peter into life that really is life. We will see what being a disciple looks like through the eyes of St. Peter and how his vision that was once buried deep down below comes to the surface and is revealed in our life: *Vivatis in Christo!* May you live in Christ!

Rev. Robert T. Jennings

For Reflection and Discussion

Return to the excavation and the floor plan, which depicts what the early Christian church appeared like underneath the Vatican.
- --what might it be like to worship under the threat of persecution?
- --do you know a Christian who has been persecuted?
- --what would motivate you to worship in the midst of these threats?
- --have you experienced power in worship? How would you describe this power?
- --what would you think if Peter said to you, "May you live in Christ"?

Measuring spiritual growth is different from measuring other forms of growth. Why?
- --what does change have to do with spiritual growth?
- --have you changed or are you growing spiritually? How so?
- --what is the difference between a spiritually immature and a spiritually mature person? How do you classify yourself? Based on what criteria?
- --are you aware of God entering your life and bringing about change?

As you reflect on the vision Peter had for the early church, take a moment and think about the vision you have for your life.
- --can you describe the vision you have for your life?
- --why is this vision important to you?
- --have you always had this vision for your life?
- --if this vision is new, when did you discover it?
- --compare the vision for your life with Peter's vision: "May you live in Christ!"

Jesus says to Peter, "Follow me." It marks the beginning of Peter's spiritual growth and cast a vision for his life.
- --what does it mean to "follow" Jesus? Where might Jesus lead us?
- --do you consider yourself to be a disciple of Jesus?
- --does the double helix of grace and knowledge relate to your spiritual growth?

Part One
Receiving the Vision

1
Everything

"His divine power has given us everything for life..."

(2 Peter 1:3)

Look at Peter and John. They are running to the tomb. They have been told the tomb is empty. How can that be? Jesus was crucified. He was dead. He had been buried in the tomb. Imagine what was racing through the minds of these two disciples. And think not just of their minds, but picture their pounding hearts and their weary souls and, yes, their tired feet as they ran to the tomb.

Look at their eyes. They do not have a look of fear. Nor do they appear as if they are running away from someone. They look intense. They look focused. What is going on clearly is not of this world. Once they arrive at the tomb, they see something in there. They see the linen shroud and the cloth that had been on Jesus's head rolled up in a corner of the tomb. Yet look again: their eyes see something big—far bigger—than they ever imagined or thought possible. They see everything now.

In one sense, I will grant you, the two disciples saw nothing in this world. But don't you see? When they stooped down and looked into the emptiness of the tomb, they saw everything as it had been told to them by Jesus. What this vision meant would radically change and transform their lives in this world as they knew it.

The empty tomb and the resurrection of Jesus provide a vision of a life like never before. It is a vision of the kingdom of God that is revealed by faith. Recall when Jesus said, "I am the resurrection and the life. Those who believe in me, even though they die, will live, and everyone who lives and believes in me will never die. Do you believe this?" (John 11:25-26).

Rev. Robert T. Jennings

Early on the first day of the week, while it was still dark, Mary Magdalene came to the tomb and saw that the stone had been removed from the tomb. So she ran and went to Simon Peter and the other disciple, the one whom Jesus loved, and said to them, "They have taken the Lord out of the tomb, and we do not know where they have laid him." Then Peter and the other disciple set out and went toward the tomb. The two were running together, but the other disciple outran Peter and reached the tomb first. He bent down to look in and saw the linen wrappings lying there, but he did not go in. Then Simon Peter came, following him, and went into the tomb. He saw the linen wrappings lying there, and the cloth that had been on Jesus's head, not lying with the linen wrappings but rolled up in a place by itself. Then the other disciple, who reached the tomb first, also went in, and he saw and believed; for as yet they did not understand the scripture, that he must rise from the dead. Then the disciples returned to their homes.

John 20:1-10

Well…do you?

Faith means so much, but here at the tomb, eternal life simply and profoundly means we can rely on Jesus and we can rely on his word. Jesus is reliable. The resurrection is for real. Everything Jesus said about the kingdom of God is true. The resurrection is not just about something that happened to one man a long, long time ago. With faith, we now see that his resurrection opens for us—Peter and John, you and me—the vision to stand on the unshakeable ground of God's kingdom where we enjoy everything in Christ. It is an abundant life. It is available right now.

Vivatis in Christo! May you live in Christ!

Growth Point—Everything

As we begin our thinking about living in Christ, a vision for this life is first spoken by Peter: "His divine power has given us everything needed for life…" (2 Peter 1:3). The focus is on the word "everything." God gives us everything? What about hunger and war and suffering and all the evil that is in the news every day? Everything?

I was in a parking lot one day and saw a bumper sticker that said "I believe in nothing." I was at first amused. It got me thinking that the person actually does believe in something by professing a belief in nothing. Then I thought, does the person not believe in him or herself? Is that person nothing? Behind the bumper sticker was probably an atheist or agnostic, but still I felt sad for the person.

God wants us to have a big vision for life, one that is greater than death. The vision lies in the 23rd psalm: "The Lord is my shepherd…I shall not want." God has given us everything needed for life when he is our shepherd. We shall not want.

It is not that God has given us just a few things needed for life. God has given us everything—all things—needed and necessary for our life in Christ. There is in the vision wholeness and completeness that is discovered in being given everything. Nothing is left out. But again, how can this be when there is so much scarcity, incompleteness, and tragedy that surrounds us and is within us? Be assured, God has given us everything needed for our life in Christ—that means God has given us everything necessary to live a Christian life in his kingdom. In God's kingdom there is no scarcity. In God's kingdom there is no loss or suffering or tragedy.

I remember leading a retreat for our church at the nearby Abbey of Gethsemane outside of Louisville, Kentucky. There at the abbey, we listened to and reflected with the guest master, Father Jacob. As we considered our life in Christ, he told us that there are only three essential questions that we need to wrestle with while on this earth. Who am I? What do I have? What do I need? These three questions, he promised, when answered, will cut to the heart and soul of all that matters.

After pausing for a moment and allowing the silence to speak, Father Jacob asked if we would like to know the answers to the three questions. He promised he could save us a great deal of time and frustration and energy. In unison, we assured the monk that we wanted the answers to those questions and we wanted them right then. From his perspective, I am sure the old monk saw us as just another compulsive, type-A, high-maintenance group trying to grab hold of God quickly before we went on about our important business at the gift shop. But what he said has stuck with me:

> Who am I? *A child of God!*
> What do I have? *Everything!*
> What do I need? *Nothing!*

This takes us back to Peter and his word: "His divine power has given us everything needed for life…" As Christians, that is our vision, which is given to us by God. This vision is received by God's grace and blesses us by helping us remove the veil between heaven and earth and see through the darkness and into the light of God's kingdom.

Vision for the Kingdom

As we take a look into the kingdom of God, we are not window shopping or picking and choosing what we like and what we don't like. No, this vision of God's kingdom is our starting place. It has everything needed for our life in Christ. The vision begins for us with Peter and John running to the empty tomb, and as we run with them, it is as if we see with fresh eyes a sign outside of the empty tomb that says "Begin here!"

The vision, of course, is less about eyesight than wisdom and insight. In fact, the spiritual life and the accompanying spiritual vision ironically often are based on what is not seen. The writer of Hebrews says, "Faith is the assurance of things hoped for, the conviction of things not seen" (Hebrews 11:1). God gives us a sixth sense.

It is this sense, however, that makes the most sense, because in this vision of God's kingdom, we become "participants of the divine nature" (2 Peter 1:4). To be specific, it means that we have faith in Jesus Christ as Lord over all of life. Out of this faith, we receive a vision for peace and hope and joy and love. It is this sixth sense that becomes the primary sense because it makes sense out of our lives by informing and shaping all our other senses. With grace, life is now not about nothing but about participating with God in everything.

We, searching for the things of God's kingdom, are like the merchant in search of fine pearls. On finding the one pearl of great value, the merchant sells all that he has and buys it (Matthew 13:45-46). So it is, Jesus tells us, with God's kingdom. It is worth more than anything else we can find. What we find in God's kingdom is eternal. Life with God is peace and hope and joy and love forever. In fact, Jesus reminds us that it is here in this kingdom we find treasures that will not rust and moths cannot consume and thieves cannot break in and steal.

In other words, nobody can take away your love for God. Nothing can destroy your peace with God. There is no illness that can rob you of hope. Sure, the psalmists say "there is weeping at night," but don't ever, ever forget, "joy comes in the morning" (Psalm 30).

God in All

Jesus did not preach that his kingdom would be found in the next life. He did not preach a message of "wait and see." No, Jesus preached the kingdom of God is near. He then said, "Repent and believe" (Mark 1:15).

Notice the order: repent first, then believe. Repent first, then see. Repent, and then live in Christ. Repentance comes first. Repentance is operative. In order to cast a vision of God's kingdom, we begin first with repentance. One way of being open to God, who is at work in everything—is to repent.

Repentance is a loaded word. Most people have negative, guild-laden thoughts when they hear the word *repentance*. That is not all bad, but just feeling guilty will not help us see the Kingdom. The Kingdom is not about negative thinking. No, *repentance* comes from the Greek word *metanoia,* which quite literally means to turn around. Yes, we repent of our sin. But what is sin? Look at sin as a driving force that separates us from God and keeps us from participating in his divine nature.

I was once told by a wise man, "If you can't find God, go back to where you have lost him." When we repent, we turn around and look for God and go back to where we lost him. We seek God by looking for why we lost him and how we lost him. After all, God has more force than sin. God has greater power than sin. Sin is strong; God is stronger. In turning around and seeking God, we are aware that as a result of sin, we have lost our direction. We cannot find meaning or purpose or value in life because of sin. So we repent. We turn around and look at what we find. God in all.

The late author Gerald May was a spiritual director of mine, and he opened for me a new dimension found in the importance of repentance. Repentance is not only a process of turning around, but in addition, May understood it as a desire to recover what has been lost. Again, think of the parables of the lost coin, the lost sheep, and the prodigal son. When we repent, we recover what has been lost. Repentance is an important step in recovery. When we repent, we recover the double helix of grace and knowledge. We recover God, whose presence can be found in everything.

So how do we repent? One way is to confess. Confession is good for the soul. Repression is not good for the soul. Repentance and confession go hand in hand. As we turn around and recover our lost relationships with God, we become aware of our deep need for God and the fact that "nothing can separate us." We become more honest with ourselves and, more importantly, more honest to God. And as this new level of honesty emerges through our confessions, we also begin to see the truth.

Yes, the truth hurts. But also don't forget Jesus's words "…if you continue in my word, you are truly my disciples, and you will know the truth and the truth will make you free!" (John 8:31). Of course, all too often we hear the part only about being free and neglect the emphasis of continuing in Jesus's word. So as we seek a vision for the Kingdom, the need to "repent" is the first word we see as we learn about becoming his disciples and recognizing his presence.

Who Do You Say that I Am?

Jesus took his disciples on a journey to the area of Caesarea Philippi. As they walked, they came to the foot of Mount Hermon. There on the side of the mountain were small places of worship dedicated to the cult of the god Pan. It was a place of immorality. Pan lived in the wilderness and loved the wild country and the mountains, and his presence in the statuary on stone niches in the side of the mountain was a distraction for the disciples.

Pan was considered to be the god of fertility who brought a new, distorted life. Pan was a lusty, playful god, and in many respects he was considered the god of instinct or the god of the inner life. Pan's worshippers not only did what was wrong but they approved of what was wrong. In fact, today our use of the word *panic* is derived from the god Pan, whose darkness could overcome people in desolate, lonely places just like the spot where the disciples were now standing. Panic and fear are the opposite of faith.

As Jesus looked before him, at the base of the mountain was a large, dark opening. Water rushed down this hole in the darkness and it revealed a bottomless pit. Large, jagged rocks surrounded the opening, appearing almost like gates. What might emerge out of the darkness depended upon Pan, or so some people imagined. The dark hole and the rocks were called the "gates of Hades," and these gates, when opened, supposedly released the forces of darkness, evil, and the underworld that housed the demonic god of death, Satan.

At this point and place, Jesus turned to the disciples and said, "Who do you say that I am?" The disciples were caught off guard and they stumbled for an answer.

Peter jumped in and proclaimed, "You are the Messiah, the son of the Living God" (Matthew 16:15-16).

To this, Jesus said, "You are Peter and on this rock I will build my church," and then, pointing to the dark hole in the side of the mountain, Jesus said, "The gates of Hades will not prevail against the church." Jesus said to Peter, "I will give you the keys of the Kingdom."

This affirmation of Peter was future oriented. Yes, Peter had momentary insight to see not only that Jesus was greater than Pan but that it was Jesus who is the living God and who has power over the gates of darkness and death and fear and all that separates us from God. Yes, for the moment, Peter's confession closed the gates of Hades, silenced Pan, and put Satan in his place.

> From that time on, Jesus began to show his disciples that he must go to Jerusalem and undergo great suffering at the hands of the elders and chief priests and scribes, and be killed, and on the third day be raised. And Peter took Jesus aside and began to rebuke Jesus, saying, "God forbid it, Lord! This must never happen to you." But Jesus turned to Peter and said to him, "Get behind me, Satan! You are a stumbling block to me; for you are setting your mind not on divine things but on human things." (Matthew 16:21-23)

Stepping Stone—Repent

What happened? In one sense, it looks like in the end, Pan and panic won. It appears as if the gates of Hades opened and, for the moment, Satan was set loose on Peter. It doesn't look good. Everything had gone so well. Everything was given to Peter. Everything in his life was at peace with God. Then in a flash it changed. Something was missing. Here is the stepping stone for Peter and for us.

When Jesus first called Peter by the Sea of Galilee to follow him, all Jesus said was, "Repent, for the kingdom of heaven is at hand" (Matthew 4:17). That was all Peter needed then. That is all Peter needed then and that is all we need now. Repent and allow God to work where we are weak. When we are aware of God working, we notice God is active, we work and we grow and we find that we are able to do what we normally cannot do on our own. The way we grow with God is by grace and doing things, thinking things, and imagining things we could never do on our own. With God's grace, we receive a vision of his divine nature, a vision of everything in which "for God, all things are possible" (Matthew 19:26), even the reality of being raised on the third day.

Repent first, then believe. Sometimes that is all we need to know. For Peter, standing there on the rock of his confession, holding the keys to the Kingdom, he knew what he was about to lose. He also knew he needed to set his mind on divine things. The beginning of spiritual growth involves turning around and receiving what has been lost. It starts with the word *metanoia:* repent. Repent is a word that will grow in Peter's life and ultimately help him see the vision of participating in the divine nature. Like keys to the Kingdom, Peter will be given the vision of everything for life in Christ.

The first step is to repent. Then everything needed for life will appear.

Rev. Robert T. Jennings

For Reflection and Discussion

GROWTH POINT—Everything

Look again at the painting by Eugène Burnand of Peter and John running to the empty tomb. Can you imagine?
- --what might they have been running from? What are they running to?
- --in your mind, what do they see?
- --what do you think they said to others when they returned home?
- --how does this vision of life eternal change the way you think?
- --in what ways does eternal life change the way you live—today?

Peter wrote that Christ has "given us everything for life" (II Peter 1:3).
- --why do you think the resurrection provides us with everything?
- --how does the resurrection open us to life in the Kingdom?
- --what does the kingdom of God provide that this world does not?
- --can you describe the kind of "treasures" found in the kingdom of God?
- --what might it mean to "lay up treasures in heaven" (Matthew 6:20)?

STEPPING STONE—Repent

Jesus preached a message to "repent and believe" (Mark 1:15).
- --what does *repent* mean to you? Is *repent* part of your everyday vocabulary?
- --Gerald May views repentance as "recovering what is lost." What is recovery?
- --can you describe something that is missing in your life?
- --how might Gerald May's description fit with our seeing God in "everything"?
- --why did Jesus rebuke Peter? What did Peter need to repent?
- --what do you make of the sequence: repent first—then believe?

2
Glory

God has called us through his own glory

(2 Peter 1:3)

The brightness of Christ leaps from this painting by Raphael. It is a painting of the Transfiguration (Luke 9:28-36). We are in overload as we look. We are not the only ones who see more than we can possibly take in. Look at the three disciples with eyes covered, Peter and James and John. They cover their eyes for the simple reason that "God is light and in him there is no darkness at all" (I John 1:5). They are in awe and wonder in the presence and brightness of God.

Words are unable to contain not only what is swirling around outside them but also what is taking place within. Imagine what was going on in Peter's mind. Only a few days ago, Peter confessed that Jesus was indeed the Messiah there at the worship site of Pan and at the gates of hell. Then Jesus spoke of being killed. Peter could not get his mind around such a thought. What good is a dead messiah? How on earth could Jesus say such a thing? Such a thought was life threatening. All Peter could say and blurt out at the time was "God forbid it, Lord!"

His reaction seemed appropriate. But Jesus turned and said to Peter, "Get behind me, Satan." Was Jesus saying that to Peter or to Satan, who had broken loose from the underworld where the gates of hell had opened? All Peter knew was the need to repent. As he fell to the ground there on top of the mountain, he shielded his eyes. So much was going on. Years later, he would write as an eyewitness who with James and John saw "majestic glory" (2 Peter 1:17). He saw Jesus reveal the glory of God. He saw and participated in the divine nature of Jesus.

Now, about eight days after these sayings, Jesus took with him Peter and John and James and went up on the mountain to pray. And while he was praying, the appearance of his face changed, and his clothes became dazzling white. Suddenly they saw two men, Moses and Elijah, talking to him. They appeared in glory and were speaking of his departure, which he was about to accomplish at Jerusalem. Now Peter and his companions were weighed down with sleep; but since they had stayed awake, they saw his glory and the two men who stood with him. Just as they were leaving him, Peter said to Jesus, "Master, it is good for us to be here; let us make three dwellings, one for you, one for Moses, and one for Elijah"—not knowing what he said. While he was saying this, a cloud came and overshadowed them, and they were terrified as they entered the cloud. Then from the cloud came a voice that said, "This is my Son, my Chosen; listen to him!" When the voice had spoken, Jesus was found alone. And they kept silent and in those days told no one any of the things they had seen.

Luke 9:28-36

The word *glory* almost defies explanation, but that is fitting for the story of the Transfiguration and for what Peter saw and for what Raphael painted. Glory has to do with honor and praise, to be sure. We live in a culture that glorifies athletes and celebrities, as examples, and we set them apart for an accomplishment or for a victory or a great performance. But the use of the word *glory* when describing the Transfiguration has a far, far greater dimension. It is not about winning or losing or stardom. It is more about light and life and a heightened awareness of God's presence. *Glory* is a religious term used to express the way in which we see the very presence of God in our lives and here on earth. Ezekiel first talked about the glory of God (Ezekiel 1:28), and he refers to having seen the glory of God move from the Temple toward where his people were in exile.

When Moses climbed Mount Sinai, the glory of the Lord appeared like a "devouring fire" (Exodus 24:17). Zechariah and Isaiah and the psalmists all give glory to God for his presence. Giving God the glory changes, transforms, and pivots the way we think and act as we become aware that God is not simply watching us but God is now present with us. When Christ's birth was announced, the word we heard from the angels and shepherds was "glory." And yes, as John writes, "We have seen his *glory*, glory as of the father's only son, full of grace and truth" (John 1:14). How do we recognize God's glory and God's presence? "Repent," as Peter was told, and watch as the glory of the Transfiguration follows. "Repent," we are told, and watch as glory reveals the divine majesty of Jesus. *Repent* sometimes can simply mean "get out of the way." *Repent* can simply mean "give God the stage for a minute." And so it is for Peter and for all of us who are on the mountain. We hear the word not only to repent but to look—look at God's glory revealed in Jesus Christ.

Growth Point—Glory

So where have you seen God's glory in your life? Think about what glory means to you. I always witness God's glory while walking a beach and simply seeing the waves roll in and out. For others, God's glory is sitting at the foot of a never-changing mountain. Many parents experience God's glory at the birth of a child.

One mother recently told me of an everyday experience of driving in the car with her child. Her mind was on her driving, on what was next on her agenda, on what had occurred during the day, and a million other things. Suddenly, from the back seat of the car, sitting in a car seat, her child shouted out, "Look, Mommy, at the sky." As the mother looked out her windshield, she and her child witnessed together a beautiful, radiant sunset. The mother recalled how simple it was to look, and for a moment she and her child felt wrapped in God's beauty. Had she not looked, she would have missed a remarkable moment, or as she reflected later, she would have missed a vision of God's glory.

Glory has to do with wonder and awe. Today, in fact, many people use the word *awesome*. The experience of wonder and awe opens us to this sense of glory and the beauty found in God's radiance. Think again of the astronauts, how time and again they look at planet Earth from their perspective in space and how, for a moment, they feel as if they have touched the majesty and glory of God.

Yes, after the disciples saw glory on the Mount of Transfiguration, life was quite simply never the same again. There was no turning back to the way life had been. From then on, it was only about the way life would be as a result of the glory they saw: "…we have seen his glory, the glory as the father's only son, full of grace and truth" (John 1:14). The Mount of Transfiguration changes Jesus right before Peter's eyes, but watch how the Transfiguration now changes Peter and our own lives.

Listen to Him!

While Jesus was praying, "he was transfigured before them, and his face shone like the sun, and his clothes became dazzling white" (Luke 9:29). One way of looking at the Transfiguration is to see that, while praying, Jesus became transparent. That is, the disciples could see through Jesus. They could see God through Jesus. They could see through Jesus all that separates the kingdom of God from the earth.

The thin veil of heaven was pulled back by Jesus momentarily, and the disciples could then see Moses and Elijah, the Law and the Prophets, right before their eyes.

This vision gathers the disciples up as they hear Jesus being strengthened "for a time of departure" (Luke 9:31), an exodus to lead his people to *the* promised land, the kingdom of God where heaven and earth are full of God's glory—forever. As we gaze at this majestic glory that emanates from the cloud, we see light and life, energy, power, goodness, and enlightenment. Where there is glory, there is a glow. It is no wonder that Jesus glows in the painting, but Jesus is not the only one who glows.

As Peter sees through Jesus in the transparency of prayer, Moses and Elijah now glow in the same circle of majestic glory. God told Moses on Mount Sinai, "You cannot see my face; for no one can see me and live" (Exodus 33:20). Instead, God gave Moses two tablets of stone with commandments and the law of the covenant. When Moses came down from the mountain, his face was shining and the glory of the Lord was reflected in the glow about him. Now we see Moses and the law in the light of Jesus, and the law is fulfilled and a new covenant is given.

Recall, God came to Elijah at a time of great spiritual desolation. Elijah was a man on the run from the wicked Queen Jezebel, and God spoke to Elijah in a "still small voice" (I Kings 19:12). The voice gave energy, life, and power to Elijah's depleted soul so that from desolation he would enter the light of consolation and climb into a chariot of fire and travel all the way to heaven. Elijah had arrived. Now we see Elijah and all the prophets in light of Jesus and their prophecies are fulfilled. The still small voice cracks like thunder. The Sermon on the Mount awakens Peter like a dream: "Do not think I have come to abolish the Law and the Prophets; I have not come to abolish but fulfill" (Matthew 5:17).

Peter's mind could not keep up with the action swirling on around and within him—nor could his mouth. There are times our words get out in front of our thoughts. This was one of those times for Peter: "Peter said to Jesus, 'Master, let us make three dwellings, one for you, one for Moses, and one for Elijah'—not knowing what he said" (Luke 9:33). Some who read this story consider Peter to have been impetuous or impulsive or believe that this was a desire on his part to house God's glory and catch fire in a bottle. What Luke clearly states, however, is Peter did not know what he said. There are times our bodies lead without our knowing. There are times we do things and say things that feel as if we have put our foot in our mouth.

The Transfiguration is not about creating dwelling places for God. God is present on earth not so his divinity may dwell in a place separate and apart from our being—no, the disciples are to become tabernacles. We are to become tabernacles, dwelling places, so that Jesus can dwell in us and we can dwell in him. Our bodies are to house the Holy Spirit. The body is to be "the temple of the Holy Spirit" so that we may live in and participate in the divine life of Christ. "Abide in me," Jesus says, "as I abide in you" (John 15:4).

The majestic glory of God thunders this point home in a message that reverberates across time and space and memory: "This is my Son, my chosen; listen to him" (Luke 9:35). Listen to him. Listen, Peter. You have two ears and one mouth for a reason. Listen. Hearing opens us to receive the external world and experiences and sounds by bringing all of this on the outside into our lives and into our souls on the inside. Inside, we begin to make sense of it—life literally becomes sensible as we listen.

When we listen, we build a tabernacle, a dwelling place, and with Peter we receive the vision for our life in Christ found in obedience. Our eyes are open to receive God's glory; our ears are open. Now on the Mount of the Transfiguration, the growth point for Peter is seeing God's glory, and the stepping stone to glory is listening. When we listen, our hearts are open through grace to see this majestic glory and receive the vision of our life in Jesus Christ. When we listen, we become aware. Our awareness is heightened not only on the outside but obviously on the inside. Listen.

Listening and Obedience

Think through the power of the words that now come to the surface of Peter's mind and are dwelling in the formation of his character. *Obedience*, for example, is not a favorite word for many people in our day and age. The mere mention of the word *obey* sounds restrictive, oppressive, and limiting. However, the opposite of the word *obey* is to disobey. We have already seen how Peter experienced this disobedience in subtle, unforeseen ways, with his body and his mouth and his mind in disobedience by not working together. It happened outside of Caesarea Philippi, and now it happened just moments ago on the Mount of the Transfiguration. Peter was not being intentionally disobedient. Here, in the unintentional area of Peter's life, God is at work, and we see Peter's spiritual growth and the formation and development of his life in Christ. Ideas have consequences, and from the cloud, the idea of "listen to him" has consequences. Listening is a stepping stone that paves the way as we become increasingly aware of God's glory found in his presence that the Spirit reveals to us. Listening is a form of obedience. Listening can help us get out of the way so God can lead us on the way.

Obedience is derived from the word *audire*, which means "to listen." Familiar words like *audio* and *audible* come from this word, as does the word *audit*. Now, which word creates the most shivers up your spine? When God says to listen, it is not like soft elevator music, nor is it in one ear and out the other. God's word is more like an audit. It is more closely aligned with a sense of deep accountability. When God speaks, we listen, and we are obedient in our minds, bodies, souls, and hearts.

Not to listen, not to be attentive to God, is a form of spiritual disobedience. The opposite of listening or hearing is *surdus*, which means "deaf." The word *absurd* is reflected when we turn a deaf ear to God. Life is absurd when we do not listen and when we do not obey. Think for a moment if you:

…did not stop at a stop light and disobeyed the rules of the road

…ran through a scanner at an airport and disobeyed the laws of travel

...mixed prescription medicines and disobeyed the instructions

...smoked a cigarette in a building, disobeying the signs that prohibited smoking

Believe it or not, these examples of disobedience were all in this morning's news! Obviously, we could identify countless other examples of disobedience through the day in our own lives that put ourselves and others at risk.

For the most part, we prefer lives of obedience. Rather than go the route of absurdity or disobedience, certainly Peter continues to grow in his obedience to Christ as God brings Peter's intentions more in line with the vision of glory. The Gospels close the account of the Transfiguration by writing that the disciples came down from the mountain and were "silent and in those days told no one any of the things they had seen" (Luke 9:36). One of the reasons for not talking is that they were now listening. They were becoming obedient. They were becoming more intentional about their life in Christ. The Gospel of John reminds us that we beheld his glory and it was filled with grace and truth. Through Peter's eyes, we see the majestic glory of Jesus, because we listen now and we are obedient to a higher authority.

Obedience to a Higher Authority

Look again at the painting of the Transfiguration by Raphael. To this point, we have only focused our attention on the top half of the painting. It is in the top half that Jesus is revealed in the majestic glory surrounded by Moses and Elijah and the kingdom of heaven. It is a brilliant painting not only because of the light coming out of the cloud but because of the brightness of ideas and images and the thoughts that are so clearly communicated for the mind to absorb. The disciples are dazzled by the presence of God, and they cover their eyes from the radiant light and energy and power that cover and overshadow the earth. That is the top half of the painting.

In the bottom half of the painting, Raphael tells the story of the day after the Transfiguration. He paints a picture that is worth a thousand words. As Jesus and the disciples descend the mountain, it is as if they are descending into hell. The top half of the painting and the scene of the Transfiguration opens our eyes to the heaven that lies about us. It is pleasant, beautiful, and glorious to look at. However, Raphael does not want us to miss the rest of the story. He does not want us to neglect the side of life that is not so beautiful and that is out of control and in a state of disorder. The painting depicts the crowd, and we can see the disheveled nature of the people, the frantic look in some eyes, and the boy who appears deranged. In contrast to the light above is the darkness now below as Jesus and the disciples step into a scene that is wild and furious and demonic.

> On the next day, when they had come down from the mountain, a great crowd met him. Just then, a man from the crowd shouted, "Teacher, I beg you to look at my son; he is my only child. Suddenly a spirit seizes him, and all at once he shrieks. It convulses him until he foams at the mouth; it mauls him and will scarcely leave him. I begged your disciples to cast it out, but they could not." Jesus answered, "You faithless and perverse generation, how much longer must I be with you and bear with you? Bring your son here." While he was coming, the demon dashed him to the ground in convulsions. But Jesus rebuked the unclean spirit, healed the boy, and gave him back to his father. And all were astounded at the greatness of God. While everyone was amazed at all that he was doing, he said to his disciples, "Let these words sink into your ears: The Son of Man is going to be betrayed into human hands." But they did not understand this saying; its meaning was concealed from them, so that they could not perceive it. And they were afraid to ask him about this saying. (Luke 9:37-43)

The report from the father of the possessed boy is clear, concise, and gruesome. A demon has overtaken his son to the point that the boy goes into convulsions and foams at the mouth, and the demon mauls the boy and will scarcely leave him. It would be tempting to interpret this story and diagnose the disorder through the eyes of a modern-day physician or psychiatrist, but one point we do not want to overlook is the complaint made by the father of the demon-possessed boy: "I begged your disciples to cast out the demon, but they could not" (Luke 9:40). The father and the boy are powerless. The disciples are powerless. The story and the painting reveal the limits of our mortal life. "They could not…" is an expression of our human limitation. It is here within the context of our vulnerability the demonic side of life enters. It is here spiritual warfare takes place. Here is where we find the battle between right and wrong, good and bad, healthy and destructive, conscious and unconscious, faithful and perverse all pictured immediately following the Transfiguration.

Take a moment and consider the demon. The nature of a demon is always destructive. That is how a demon destroys and diminishes mortal life. *Diabolis,* the devil, is the opposite of *symbolis.* A symbol pulls meaning together. The diabolis breaks meaning apart. Before us is a story of meaning and purpose and direction. It is a battle of the spirits. On one side is the demon, who is unable to be constructive, much less creative, because the demonic is separated from the source of creativity found ultimately in the creator. As we see the story unfold before our eyes, the demon strikes terror inappropriately and irresponsibly, using fear and evil and death as weapons. It is Beelzebub, "the father of lies," the devil, who tells the father the disciples cannot cast out the demon.

Jesus comes down from the mountain of Transfiguration and descends into this hell. Jesus is "the way and the truth and the life." (John 14:6) He is the one with whom God is well pleased. "Listen to him," we were told on top of the mountain. It should be no different now at the bottom of the mountain. In Christ, we find meaning and purpose and direction wherever we are located. By living in Christ and by participating in his divine nature, we dwell in him and he dwells within us. Rather than build a tabernacle to house Jesus, he enters our life so "he is with us always." (Matthew 28:20) He is the living symbol or the unifying, coherent source with whom God is well pleased. His spiritual nature brings order to our human nature. To our human limitation, we discover through divine participation with him an unlimited source of grace. As we listen to him, we allow his word to enter our life and the glory of the transfiguration shines now even or especially in some of the darkest places in our life.

So, Jesus casts out the demon, heals the boy, and gives him back to his father. "And all were astounded at the greatness of God" (Luke 9:43). It sounds like a perfect ending to a great story. God wins. The devil loses. But there is more. "While everyone was amazed at all that he was doing, he said to his disciples, "Let these words sink into your ears. The Son of Man is going to be betrayed into human hands." (Luke 9:44) Listen. The spiritual war is not over.

Listen to him when we are on the top of the mountain, or when we are living through hell. God's glory will shine through regardless of our circumstances if we let his words sink into our ears.

Stepping Stone—Listen

The Transfiguration gave Peter a glimpse into the Kingdom and the majestic glory of God. By listening to Jesus, he would spiritually grow. He would become aware of God's glory. And by listening, we become aware of our surroundings and God's glory.

When my father died, after being crippled for years by Alzheimer's, I was the only one with him as he breathed his last. I was struck by the silence, and yet I was aware of the sense of holiness, that something big was going on. It wasn't just death. It really was life. All of Dad's life was before me.

Moments after he died, there was a knock at the door. It was an unwelcome interruption by housekeeping. I informed the cleaning lady that my dad just died. She apologized for interrupting and then expressed her condolences. I waited for her to leave. Instead, she approached Dad's bed and asked me if she could say a prayer. She did not know I was a minister, but I can't tell you how grateful I was to have someone with me and praying for my dad. I told her to please feel free to pray.

She did. I can honestly tell you she prayed like an angel. She prayed that the spirit of God would enter Dad right then. She prayed that the Spirit would breathe for Dad in ways that he no longer could. She asked God to enter his feet that could no longer walk and hold firm his hands that were at rest. She prayed that God would be in his eyes so that he could see his loved ones on earth as were those in heaven. On she prayed, and I just wept like a baby. There was glory that surrounded Dad that day.

And I didn't say a word. I kept my mouth shut. All I did was listen and obey the little lady from housekeeping. Here is something else I will never forget. This took place on the Sunday we were celebrating the day of the Transfiguration.

May You Live in Christ!

For Reflection and Discussion

GROWTH POINT—Glory
Look at the painting by Raphael. What do you make of Jesus, the light, the cloud, and what Peter describes as the "Majestic glory"?
--what do you know about glory?
--can you identify a time when you experienced glory in your life?
--would you consider that time a spiritual experience?
--what did it have to do with God?

Place yourself for a moment in the painting with Peter on top of the mountain.
--what do you think your reaction would be?
--how might you respond to the experience?
--what most catches your attention?
--Peter wants to build a "tabernacle." What would an inner tabernacle be like?
--what do you think the healing story and the Transfiguration have in common?

STEPPING STONE—Listen
As you reflect on the way glory entered your life, do you recall listening?
--do you consider yourself to be a good listener?
--in what ways does listening contribute to your inner tabernacle?
--what areas of your life need attention? Where do you need to listen?
--has listening helped you see God's glory in your life?

God speaks from out of a cloud and says to Peter, "Listen!"
--what might this mean for Peter as they walk back to join the disciples?
--how does the act of listening help deepen our awareness of others?
--what do you know about listening to Jesus?
--how does this act of listening open you to see God's glory?

3
Faith

Make every effort to add to your faith
(2 Peter 1:5)

Faith is the name of the game. It is what we are all about. Faith is the foundation upon which our spiritual life in Christ grows. Faith provides us with a vision that can see into the invisible world of the kingdom of God. Faith informs everything we do, and everything we think and feel and choose.

Today, however, contemporary society often views faith as something that is detached from thinking, or as beyond our wildest dreams, or as somehow separated or removed from reality, and considers faith to be little more than believing in something that isn't so. Of course, for the believer, faith is just the opposite. It is like the law of gravity. Faith is our foundation. It gets us out of bed in the morning and enables us to stand and face the day. Faith is personal, to be sure. Faith is *in* the person of Jesus Christ.

Like gravity, however, faith can be something we do not always think about. Faith can be taken for granted. Peter calls our attention to this danger when he writes *"make every effort to add to your faith."*

Notice Peter does not write "make every effort to *earn* your faith." Faith is a gift that is given to us by grace. Faith is something we receive. Faith is truly a miracle. For some, faith is discovered overnight or in a flash. For others, it is a gradual process of repentance and discovery and obedience and revelation. Regardless, faith is not earned. It does, however, take effort to support it. Think of the story of Peter climbing out of a boat and trying to walk on water. We will look at this story as a lesson in faith. Through the eyes of Peter, not only will we see faith as foundational to Peter's spiritual growth but we will also look at the miracle of faith in our lives as we make every effort to support it.

May You Live in Christ!

Immediately, he made the disciples get into the boat and go on ahead to the other side while he dismissed the crowds. And after he had dismissed the crowds, he went up the mountain by himself to pray. When evening came, he was there alone, but by this time the boat, battered by the waves, was far from the land, for the wind was against them. And early in the morning, he came walking toward them on the sea. But when the disciples saw him walking on the sea, they were terrified, saying, "It is a ghost!" And they cried out in fear. But immediately Jesus spoke to them and said, "Take heart, it is I; do not be afraid." Peter answered him, "Lord, if it is you, command me to come to you on the water." He said, "Come." So Peter got out of the boat, started walking on the water, and came toward Jesus. But when he noticed the strong wind, he became frightened, and beginning to sink, he cried out, "Lord, save me!" Jesus immediately reached out his hand and caught him, saying to him, "You of little faith, why did you doubt?" When they got into the boat, the wind ceased. And those in the boat worshiped him, saying, "Truly you are the Son of God."

Matthew 14:22-33

Walking on Water

Now look at the Delacroix painting. It's eerie. Everything is wavy. It is what makes for getting seasick. Water—waves and turbulence and wind—can be life threatening, even for fishermen like Peter and the disciples. Such conditions were part of their everyday existence. It was another day.

Seeing Jesus walking towards them on the sea—now that is a different story. Scripture records the disciples as being terrified, as if they were seeing a ghost. Having just read the story of the Transfiguration, we are aware that when Jesus prays, anything can happen. We are also aware that when Jesus prays, there is a transparency about him. We can see through him into the supernatural Kingdom that surrounds him and permeates his being. It is not about an optical illusion or some kind of magician's card trick or seeing a ghost. It is about vision.

Peter receives this vision. He recognizes Jesus, and the fact that Jesus is walking on top of the water and in control of the natural elements reveals to Peter a new reality—Jesus is the God of life!

Light surrounds the figure of Jesus in the Delacroix painting, much like the light and the majestic glory that came out of the cloud in the painting of the Transfiguration by Raphael. What the artists are expressing is not just the inexpressible but the stability that is found in the light that originates from our faith in Jesus. Compare walking in the light to stumbling in the dark. Compare a stable life to one that is unstable. It is like comparing faith to fear. Fear is most often found in falling and sinking into the abyss of nothingness.

Fear of the Unknown

One reason for this fear is seen in the painting. Peter looks like a blob. We know it is Peter only because we know the story. But the reality is, when we are falling and sinking and in the dark and unstable, there is not much to our identity. Recall the monk at Gethsemane who posed the question "Who am I?" In one sense, Peter was about to lose his identity as he became frightened and he began to sink. But in another sense, his identity in Christ is about to become secure when he cries out, "Lord, save me!"

Fear, in many respects, is the opposite of faith. Of course, "perfect love casts out fear" (I John 4:18), but what makes love perfect? Love of Christ is based on faith in Christ and reveals a complete, whole, or perfect love. Fear, on the other hand, leads to a loss of faith and makes love imperfect.

Granted, many people think doubt is the opposite of faith. Doubt, however, can be used, and it can be employed in the search for faith. Asking questions and having doubt are not necessarily a lack of faith, but rather they can be a sign of a search for faith. A little skepticism can keep us honest. Notice how Jesus says to Peter, "You of little faith, why did you doubt?" He doesn't say to Peter, "Why are you afraid?" Jesus knows why Peter is afraid. But why does he ask about doubt?

Peter was in many respects self-made. When Jesus posed the question of doubt there on the water, with the winds blowing and the waves swirling about Peter, it wasn't a trick question. Rather, Jesus was clearly concerned with the question of salvation. Do we need a savior?

Embedded in this story is a miracle. It is the miracle of salvation, being saved, being rescued, finding a power who is greater than ourselves.

The fact that Peter was frightened helps us see he was about to lose his faith as well as his life. Now one might object and ask, "Well, who wouldn't be afraid? Who wouldn't panic at the thought of drowning? Isn't Peter's reaction a natural or normal response to a life-threatening situation?" Yes, Peter is acting human. His human nature is fully engaged and totally threatened by drowning—there is no question about it. A better question, however, is "What about Peter's spiritual nature?" By asking this question, we plumb the depths with Peter, and as we go under the water, we find ourselves dying to our human nature, dying to our self-centeredness, and rising to our life that is now centered in and held by the firm grasp and in the light of our savior Jesus Christ.

Rev. Robert T. Jennings

Faith Reveals Convictions

A man in our parish made a big impression on me years ago. He was a senior executive, and I knew him mostly based on reputation. When he retired, I began to see him more at church, especially when he and his wife of fifty years weren't traveling around the world. They loved retirement, and together they were making the most of it. One day, he called to inform me his wife had been diagnosed with lung cancer. It was serious. Over the next several months, I watched as this giant of a man cared for his wife. He cooked for her, dressed her, bathed her, brushed her hair, cleaned the house, and did all the functional chores that demonstrated his overwhelming love and devotion toward her. He had no interest in calling for outside help, even though the toll that his caregiving was taking on him was apparent. His wife, a beautiful woman, died as they slept together.

With his adult children and grandchildren arriving from all around the country, there was plenty of activity to keep him going until the day of the funeral. It was then he walked into my office and told me he wanted to make a change in the service we had planned together. He wanted to speak. As young as I was, I had officiated at enough funerals to discourage his speaking, only because I thought the liturgical structure of the funeral was designed to minister and care for him. He would have none of it.

During the service, he came forward at the appropriate time. He patted the casket. Most of us began to lose it. From there, as he looked at the casket, he said, "I want you all to know that fifty-one years ago, we stood here and said we loved each other 'for better for worse, for richer or for poorer, in sickness and in health, to love and to cherish, until we are parted by death.'" Then, turning back to us, he said, "I want to thank you for being here and for celebrating with us our marriage. And I especially want to thank God here at this altar for giving me the love of my life and for helping us to fulfill these vows—today." With that he sat down.

Needless to say, I could hardly stand up and continue with the rest of the service. The impression it made on me, not only as a minister but as a husband and a father of four boys, was a lasting one. What I saw and experienced through this man was a life of stability. His stability was based on his faith, his beliefs, his values, his commitments, and most especially his convictions. Convictions are based on faith in a greater power. As great as this man appeared before my eyes, he knew his Lord was far greater. When he navigated the turbulent waters of cancer for his wife, his love for her grew deeper than the sea. Before my eyes, I saw him step out of the boat and walk with his wife, assured of an eternal love that calmed even the fear of death. Faith in the Lord is extraordinary, but be assured Jesus enters the ordinary of everyday life.

Growth Point—Faith

Faith in the Lord is the first step that leads us from a self-centered existence to a life that is now centered on Jesus, where we enter a life of extraordinary proportions. Faith does not always come easily. Faith is not something we earn or deserve or get because of what we have done. Faith is not always rational. It is not based necessarily on cause and effect. Faith is, however, reasonable, and it is held out as a gift that comes to us from God's amazing grace. When all is said and done, faith often appears as a result of our having put ourselves in position to receive faith. It is like getting ready to hit a forehand in tennis. Hips, feet, eyes, all have to be in position. Another way of being in position to receive faith is by placing our confidence in God. It is a position of trust. And for some, trust is hard to come by.

From early on, many of us were trained to put our best feet forward. We learned how to dress for success. We were taught the importance of studying hard and that a penny saved is a penny earned and the Lord helps those who help themselves and all the other teachings in *Poor Richard's Almanac*. All of that and more helped us to create and shape our own identities. They are identities that sometimes fit well within this world and within our mortal life. But they are identities for life only in this world, and only when things are going our way. When faced with failure or with death, with misinformation, with financial crisis, or with relationships that sour, what then happens to these worldly identities we have so carefully crafted and created in our minds? It is here, within the question of mortality, we begin to see the limitations and the illusions and the superficial nature of living in this world. We see as well a glimpse of the paradoxical biblical truth found by living in the world but not of it. And we desire to see a power greater than ourselves.

As Peter stepped out of the boat, he found something real about life. He sank. He could not do it alone. He needed a faith based on a new reality for living. As he was going underwater, Peter cried out for a faith that was reliable. He found in Jesus faith that he could rely on for this life and for the life to come. Faith is about living forever—and not simply dying. As Peter began to go underwater and into the darkness and abyss of nothingness, he cried out, "Lord, save me!"

Being saved is loaded with meaning. It has many expressions and experiences and many implications. What it has meant for me over the years is life, *zoe* life, the fullness of life. Salvation is not about our mortal life, but it is about our immortal nature and our life in Christ. *Vivatis in Christo!*—May you live in Christ!—is a vision that comes to mind especially as we come to the surface of the turbulent waters with Peter and suck in the supernatural air and breathe the spirit of eternal life.

Again, when we think of this vision of faith, or salvation, or spiritual growth, or grace, it all sounds nice. We want it! But don't forget the lesson of Peter…it is about first going under. There out on the water, with the waves crashing and the winds swirling and the darkness surrounding him, he stepped out on his own, with his own identity, and there was nothing "nice" about that experience. It was terrifying. His life was out of control. When he came up for air, when he came up from being underwater, when he grabbed hold of the firm hand of Jesus, he no longer was on his own but he was alive to a new identity and under the power of a new control for his life. His life, in other words, would no longer be the same. This is the process of conversion. Conversion is a change.

I have sat with many people who have hit bottom. Often, it is as a result of alcohol or drug abuse. Hitting bottom is a way of describing self-destruction. There, on the bottom of the wreckage of one's life, is a reality that it is time to seek help. In the midst of the pain of hitting bottom and in the swirling waters of a life that is out of control, the recognition and the blinding flash appear—it is impossible to save oneself.

It need not be only addiction. People in all walks of life and in all kinds of circumstances hit bottom for a wide variety of reasons. The point is we can all identify with Peter going under. The growth point comes when we realize at least there is a bottom. And the bottom is solid. It is where faith can be discovered. It is the place of conversion. It is the ground of our being. With Peter, it is here in our helplessness we cry out for help. The cry of faith is a growth point. The silence is broken. We have done all we can do. "Into your hands, O Lord, I commit my spirit" (Psalm 31:5). We surrender.

Stepping Stone—Surrender

Peter learned that night as he got back into the boat that faith in God comes to us not in our strengths, abilities, and competencies, but faith comes where there is an opening, where there is a crack in our thick skull, and usually where we are at our weakest and most vulnerable. But faith is sure and it is certain. It is something you can hold onto, rely on, stand on, and believe in, just as sure as the hand that was held out to Peter.

The story of Peter and his attempt to walk on water is not about his near drowning. It is about his being saved. People who hit bottom do not just stay there. They move on. Their lives are different. They are no longer the same as a result of being saved. I remember years ago—just like it was yesterday—flipping my van over in a ditch on a rainy day. We had hydroplaned. The van was filled with my children and my wife. It could have all been over for my entire family in a split second. Mercifully, the ditch across the highway into which we crashed was wet from the rain and cushioned the blow. We were saved. It is hard to explain. I will say I walked away from the wreck a different person. I had experienced a miracle. Faith now drives my life.

Of course, there were a million questions that followed my lying upside down in a ditch in a van filled with our screaming children. I am sure Peter had a few questions as he climbed back into the boat. For me, the accident in the van is not just an event in time. It is a timeless event. I will carry it with me always. I believe there was a hand on the steering wheel. It was not mine.

Once we have been saved, once we have experienced life with God—faith follows. Our faith may be little, but the fact is we have been saved, and that is huge. By surrendering, by turning our lives over to God, by placing our confidence in Jesus, faith begins. Every effort to support and add to our faith is now what spiritual growth is all about. The effort is graceful. For example, one way to support faith and add to faith is through goodness. Faith opens us to God's goodness.

It is in God's goodness we see the vision of life in Christ.

May You Live in Christ!

For Reflection and Discussion

GROWTH POINT—Faith

Take another look at the painting by Delacroix that introduces our chapter. Do you notice the light that surrounds Jesus? What do you make of Peter?
- --in what ways is this a picture of faith for you?
- --can you picture a time in your life when you seemed to be going under?
- --do you recall the thoughts and feelings associated with that experience?
- --did faith come to you?
- --do you have a working definition now for faith?

As you read through this chapter, you may have noticed an emphasis was placed on fear as being the opposite of faith. Does that make sense to you?
- --do you consider your faith stronger than your fears? How come?
- --in what ways has Jesus given you faith?
- --how has this faith *in* Jesus helped you to spiritually grow?
- --do you think of yourself as a different person as a result of your faith?
- --would you say that you have been "saved"? Explain.

STEPPING STONE—Surrender

Reflect for a moment on the meaning of surrender to you and your spiritual growth.
- --how has surrender brought you to faith in Christ?
- --is this dynamic of surrender something you can discuss with others?
- --what might it mean to let go and let God?
- --has faith in Jesus revealed to you a new life? How so?

When they got back into the boat, the disciples said, "Truly you are the Son of God."
- --what did they see in Jesus that elicited that statement?
- --can you recall from your faith experience when the "winds ceased"?
- --did elements like peace, joy, hope, and love follow?
- --what is the relationship between faith and a conviction?

Part Two
Seeing the Vision

4
Goodness

Make every effort to add to your faith goodness
(2 Peter 1:5)

God is good. When adding goodness to faith, it is obvious that Peter sees the two—goodness and faith—interrelated and inextricably bound together. Rather than start with an ethical discussion on goodness or the virtue of goodness, let us examine Peter's approach to goodness. By connecting goodness to faith, Peter makes it clear that the source of our goodness is God. God is good.

The word *good* is derived from *God*. God and good are synonymous. In early English, saying "goodbye" was a way of saying "God bless" or "God be with you." The same holds true with a discussion about Good Friday. It is God's Friday.

Good and God hold hands and walk together in the first chapter of Genesis and the story of creation. Count the number of times the word *good* is used. God created the light and saw the light was good. God created the sky and the waters and the earth and the vegetation and said it was good. You know the story of creation (Genesis 1). The completion came when God created man in his image. Being created in God's image does not mean we look like God outwardly, but to be created in God's image means that we have attributes and characteristics that are like God. One attribute or characteristic is that of being good. Good is like God. And we can be good because we have been created in God's image. We can imagine what it is like to be good.

Sometimes people struggle with this understanding of God being good. They do not necessarily think God is bad, but they struggle mightily with the problem of why bad things happen. The logic follows that

Rev. Robert T. Jennings

Now when Jesus heard this, he withdrew from there in a boat to a deserted place by himself. But when the crowds heard it, they followed him on foot from the towns. When he went ashore, he saw a great crowd; and he had compassion for them and cured their sick. When it was evening, the disciples came to him and said, "This is a deserted place, and the hour is now late; send the crowds away so that they may go into the villages and buy food for themselves." Jesus said to them, "They need not go away; you give them something to eat." They replied, "We have nothing here but five loaves and two fish." And he said, "Bring them here to me." Then he ordered the crowds to sit down on the grass. Taking the five loaves and the two fish, he looked up to heaven, and blessed and broke the loaves, and gave them to the disciples, and the disciples gave them to the crowds. And all ate and were filled; and they took up what was left over of the broken pieces, twelve baskets full. And those who ate were about five thousand men, besides women and children.

Matthew 14:13-21

if bad things happen, surely they must be God's fault. It is almost as if humans bear no responsibility for car wrecks or war or famine or any of the "bad" things that happen. And how do we explain when good things happen? Is it fair to bring God into the discussion?

When Goodness Enters

Recall for a moment, in 2010, the rescue of the mine workers in Chile. How beautiful, how wonderful, how thrilling, how good was it to watch the miners one by one return to the surface after seventy days of being buried alive. Yes, yes, yes, a million times a million the cry went up, "Yes!" Yes to a story of goodness.

The story of the rescued mine workers in Chile was such a life-affirming story. It was wonderful—that is, full of wonder. It was a rescue story filled with joy and goodness and with deep compassion. For days, the world was riveted as one by one the miners were brought to the surface from the mine and the darkness of death. I don't know about you, but I could not get enough of the story.

I actually, however, heard one news anchor say during a broadcast that he was concerned—at first—about devoting so much time to each rescue. He felt the repetition in the story would soon turn "boring."

What this poor anchor didn't realize is that the negative, upsetting, violence-laden death scenes that we are fed daily numb us psychologically, intellectually, and even spiritually. The bad news is what bores us. Sin numbs us and deadens us.

The story coming out of Chile was different. It was much like that a year earlier with Captain Chesley "Sully" Sullenberger and the "Miracle on the Hudson." It was thrilling! It was good news. It was about life. It was a story about a miracle. A miracle as you well know—by its very nature—implies that God has intervened in the course of our physical, material world. In fact, one miner appeared briefly before the television camera and, when asked what he thought about the other thirty-three miners, he corrected the reporter. Without blinking, he said there were thirty-four miners. God was in the mine with them.

Philosopher and prince of modern skeptics David Hume influenced a whole generation of modern thinkers to understand a miracle as a violation of natural law or an interruption of nature's regularities. His point simply asserts nature and physical reality as a closed system, one even God can't interrupt. There is a cause and there is an effect. There are laws which govern nature. But who says the universe is a closed system? Rarely will you find a serious thinker today making such a claim. The universe is evolving. There are openings. And that means, for the religious person, words like *holy, grace, prayer, faith, mystery, worship, Jesus,* and yes—*miracles*—are still fair game and part of the equation, because we believe God has the ability to intervene in our world. We see God enter our world, and therefore it is hard to look at the world the same way again. Once we have faith, we have a different vision for our lives in this world. God is present. God is with us. Emmanuel.

The investigation, then, into whether or not a miraculous event actually occurred in Chile and deep down in the darkness of that mine or on the chilly waters of the Hudson River depends upon a pattern of inquiry, a witness or testimony of individuals who experienced the miracle, and then consequences as to what happened as a result of the miracle. Were lives changed? Yes, we saw mountains moved, rivers parted, and prayers answered as we walked through the valley of the shadow of death.

"O taste and see that the Lord is good" (Psalm 34:8).

Growth Point—Goodness

James writes, "Every good endowment…is from above" (James 1:17), which in some respects is a startling statement, especially in our day and age. We are surrounded today by a prevailing sentiment and attitude that states, "I don't need God in order to be good," or "I know good people who do not believe in God." There is the belief that good deeds are simply human. But the point Peter makes and scripture witnesses to time and time again is the rock-solid belief that the source of goodness is God.

Goodness is a growth point for our faith development. By doing good works, by being a good person, by recognizing the good in others, we begin to see the fruit of goodness all around and in and through God's creation. It is not about looking at the world through those proverbial rose-colored glasses; rather, it is about becoming aware and conscious and attentive and intentional about the place of goodness in our lives. In the Sermon on the Mount, Jesus addresses this matter of goodness and the fruit of goodness by comparing a good tree to a bad tree: "A good tree cannot bear bad fruit, nor can a bad tree bear good fruit" (Matthew 7:18). It seems obvious. How often have your heard it said, when engaged with a problematic person, "Consider the source"? That is all Jesus is saying when he compares humans to trees. If we are not producing good fruit, it is not only a reflection on the fruit—something is wrong with the tree. Here, again, we need to look within, at the roots, or in the case of human beings, our hearts and souls and minds.

For this matter of goodness, Jesus calls upon his followers to prioritize: "Seek first the kingdom of God and his righteousness, and all things will be given to you as well" (Matthew 6:33). The kingdom of God is the source of goodness. Righteousness has to do with character and attributes and the image of God, which is good. Seek the source of goodness and seek the character of goodness, and it will be given to you.

This source of goodness, God, creates our world, gives us life, and adds to our faith. Our job is not to stand in judgment, separating good trees from bad trees or sheep from goats, but to "grow in grace and knowledge of our Lord and Savior" (2 Peter 3:18). One way we grow is through discernment. Discernment is a form of judgment, and it has to do with our ability to separate or cut by making wise decisions. What color tie should I wear, what food should I eat, why am I worried? Daily questions that pop up in our minds, from the sublime to the very serious, help us to examine the fruit we are bearing and to grow in the grace and knowledge of our Lord. Discernment has to do with our ability to know right from wrong, good from bad. Discernment is an important word in spiritual direction because it taps into our ability to "test everything; hold fast to what is good" (I Thessalonians 5:21). Discernment helps us separate what Paul refers to as works of the flesh from works of the spirit.

Works of the Flesh

Works of the flesh are works that are self-reliant. We think and do and live without God. God is not needed. We can handle what we need to handle without God. We are separate from God. When we need God, of course, we can always call on him. Such independence is at the heart of our works of the flesh, and it is a delusion left from the serpent. It is a form of idolatry and self-worship.

As we become increasingly self-reliant and self-aware and self-focused, we become more and more self-sufficient and self-centered into thinking all goodness springs from what we have done and what we have accomplished. Works of the flesh have to do with my achievements, my agenda, my goals, my work, my schedule, my money, ad nauseam. Peter encourages us to "escape from the corruption" (2 Peter 1:4) of the mind and the heart and the soul that comes with our misplaced desire, which Peter clearly identifies with one word: lust.

Lust is a malady and one of the deadly sins that plagues our Western culture in everything from the obsessions found in this sex-saturated environment to our lust for material goods. The rest of this book could obviously be a discussion on lust, but in reality, thinking about lust is like thinking about mud. We get dirty from mud. We get stuck in the mud. Mud is not clean. We try to stay out of the mud.

Scripture is clear about how lust blurs our vision of God and distorts our desire to please God, making us in many respects maladjusted. Jesus speaks of this when he says, "You have heard that it was said, 'You shall not commit adultery.' But I say to you that everyone who looks at a woman with lust has already committed adultery with her in his heart" (Matthew 5:28).

Paul writes about the works of the flesh by listing many of the problems that emerge from lust and from not being good: "fornication, impurity, licentiousness, idolatry, sorcery, enmities, strife, jealousy, anger, quarrels, dissensions, factions, envy, drunkenness, carousing, and things like these" (Galatians 5:19-21). It is quite a laundry list.

To this "corruption," Jesus says, "Blessed are the pure in heart" (Matthew 5:8). Purity of heart has to do with "singleness of heart" (Colossians 3:22), and it ushers in virtuous living or a wholehearted approach to life that has been set free from the works of the flesh. When we are set free and liberated from the power of lust, then as Peter writes, we "escape corruption" by "becoming participants of the divine nature" (2 Peter 1:4). So how can we escape corruption?

Here is where Peter encourages us to look at faith in Jesus as the key that unlocks us and sets us free from the corruption of the soul. Look at the miracle of faith that has entered our lives, and see how faith now brings life in Christ. Rather than focus on the mud of lust, through faith in our life in Christ, we gain clarity and have a vision of becoming participants in the divine nature. May you live in Christ! This life is made possible and guided and cleansed by the Holy Spirit.

Walking by the Spirit

The Holy Spirit brings faith in Jesus and, like a key, helps us escape the corruption of lust and the works of flesh so that we might be free to walk in the Spirit. It is here, in the Holy Spirit, we discover the fruits of the Spirit that await us. Unlike the apple in the Garden of Eden, these fruits are to be enjoyed and reflect God's nature and God's virtues. By participating in this divine nature, we walk not by works of the flesh but by the Spirit who is at work in us and who is producing such fruit as love, joy, peace, patience, kindness, goodness, gentleness, faithfulness, and self-control (Galatians 5:22-23).

Peter focuses our attention on goodness because good is a virtue of God, and it is here in the goodness of God our faith is discovered, strengthened, and revealed. Yes, of course anyone can be good. Yes, there are a lot of good people doing good things in this world. By linking goodness with faith, however, Peter raises a different understanding of what makes for a good person. A good person is by faith—alive in Christ—which means a good person draws goodness from faith. Without faith, goodness is weakened. Without goodness, we are vulnerable to lust and corruption. Goodness supports faith as the antidote to lust. Goodness fights and combats lust.

Goodness then supports this witness of faith; in fact, we are reminded "all things work together for good, for those who love God" (Romans 8:28). Since goodness is found in our faith in God who has entered our world, there is, as a result, an unlimited supply of goodness. Unlike works of the flesh, which are mortal and limited by our hands, the goodness of God is eternal. When we are with God in faith, we never tire of our desire for good. Goodness can be found in abundance. By walking in the Spirit, we walk not in the mud but "we walk in the light, as God himself is light" (I John 1:7). Our human nature gives way to our spiritual nature, which finds it natural not to hide our light under a bushel basket but to "let your light so shine before others, so that they may see your good works and give glory to your Father in heaven."

Seeing good works and letting the light shine are the polar opposite of lust and getting stuck in the mud by our works of the flesh. Goodness reflects the vision for our life in Christ, and by walking in the Spirit, we now participate in God's divine nature and support the miracle of faith that satisfies our deepest desires.

Stepping Stone—Compassion

Peter saw this vision of goodness adding to faith when he and the disciples were with Jesus in a deserted place. According to scripture, the reason for their being in that deserted place where Jesus fed the five thousand was the news they had just heard about John the Baptist. John had been arrested by King Herod, because he had been speaking out about the moral decay and the loss of goodness. John personalized and directed his prophecy towards King Herod, who had married his brother's wife out of lust. The confrontation led to a grizzly, lewd scene in which John was beheaded. Jesus went to a deserted place, a quiet place, a place of solitude, to pray and support his faith with the divine nature and goodness of God. The darkness of Herod was powerful. God's goodness is more powerful. The deserted place was symbolic of solitude with God and the escape from the corruption of the world. But Jesus wasn't the only one who wanted the goodness of God. Crowds were attracted. The deserted place, the place of solitude, was transformed into a place of healing and nurturing and goodness as Jesus began to cure many. Right before his eyes, Peter saw the goodness of God and a glimpse into the Kingdom expressed as compassion in the life of Jesus.

Compassion has to do with a love not only for God but for his people. Life, zoe life, abundant life, life that is eternal, is shared. There in the deserted place, the fullness of life in Christ and his kingdom was experienced by the crowds, and evil and indifference and cruelty were overcome. Hatred and anger and violence were replaced by goodness and compassion and love. As the crowds began to discover compassion, they found as well God's compassion and the truth to "be compassionate just as your Father is compassionate" (Luke 6:36). Compassion reflects the goodness of God.

It is easy to think of compassion as an exercise in doing good, but as you can see from this little scene or drama in the deserted place, compassion is a stepping stone for Peter and the disciples. It is a step toward the conversion of heart and mind and soul. Peter saw compassion making a difference and revealing goodness. Compassion takes us out of ourselves. We are less self-centered when we are compassionate. In fact, when we are compassionate toward another, we give of ourselves. Compassion helps us see the vision of life in Christ as we move from self-centered lives to secure, capable, responsible, and centered selves that are more concerned with others because of our faith.

Jesus saw the great crowds, and as he cured their sick, he had compassion for them. The word *compassion* is derived from the Latin *cum* and *pati*, which translated mean "to suffer with." As Jesus extended compassion to the crowds, he suffered with them here on earth and in their mortal nature. By breaking bread, he welcomed them into a spiritual nature and life with the goodness of God.

Unfortunately, Peter and the other disciples were more concerned with the time of day and their own needs, and they were less hospitable as they said to Jesus, "This is a deserted place, and the hour is now late; send the crowds away so they may go into the villages and buy food for themselves." Here is the stepping stone of compassion. Jesus simply says to their request, "They need not go away; you give them something to eat" (Matthew 14:16). You want goodness? Start with compassion in Jesus.

A Picture of Compassion

As we close our chapter, look again at the painting by Laura James. There is Jesus front and center as we the viewers now center our lives in him. The disciples are on one side. The crowd of five thousand is on the other side. He takes the five barley loaves and the two fish from the boy, and in the Eucharistic pattern of action, he blesses and breaks the bread and gives it away to the crowds. Jesus performs a miracle. The compassion, the welcome, and the hospitality in God's kingdom add to the faith that provides for the new creation, which is not corrupt but good.

This re-creation, this new life, is good, and it can be seen in the painting, where in the center is the water of life whose source is Jesus. The river represents a never-ending supply of goodness from God, which adds to our faith. Jesus is the shepherd who guides us to springs of the water of life, where the God of compassion will wipe away every tear from our eyes (Revelation 7:17). This is the vision for the abundant life and the goodness of God.

It is not a vision that comes to us naturally, but it is revealed by the Spirit, so that "out of the believer's heart shall flow rivers of living water" (John 7:38). The goodness of life in Christ is made known in the feeding of the five thousand. Knowledge of this life in Christ matters. By participating in the divine nature of Christ, Peter was learning. We learn sometimes by doing. In Peter's case—as in ours—what he was doing and learning was spiritual knowledge. It is to this knowledge we now turn.

May You Live in Christ!

For Reflection and Discussion

GROWTH POINT—Goodness

The painting by Laura James reveals the miracle of Jesus feeding the five thousand. What do you know about miracles? How does a miracle reflect God's goodness?

--where and when did you first learn the difference between bad and good?
--in your mind, what makes for a good person? Identify a good person.
--does God have something to do with his or her goodness?
--where do you see faith and goodness working together?

Stay with the painting and the miracle that literally pours goodness out of the river of life. What might the people be thinking? How about the disciples? The boy? Jesus?

--in 2 Peter 1:5, the connection is made between faith and goodness. Why?
--in what ways is the painting a picture of creation or re-creation?
--how does goodness help us to grow into the character of Christ?
--from your experience, which is stronger: lust or goodness? Which bears fruit?

STEPPING STONE—Compassion

Why did Jesus have "compassion" for the crowds? When are you likely to have compassion? When you feel like it? A certain time of the day?

--how does compassion help you locate and find goodness in your life?
--is compassion more than a decision? How would you describe compassion?
--recall an experience of compassion. Who was involved? What happened?
--does compassion take us out of ourselves? Where does compassion take us?

Rev. Robert T. Jennings

    The disciples ask that Jesus send the crowds away so they can buy food for themselves. Why?
- --are the disciples concerned with the crowds? Where are they most concerned?
- --what does Jesus teach the disciples about their concern?
- --how does compassion open our eyes to see goodness in God's kingdom?
- --is a faith community possible without compassion? What about goodness?

5
Knowledge

Make every effort to add to your faith with goodness,
and goodness with knowledge
(2 Peter 1:5)

In goodness, we find God. God is good. How do we know that? Peter encourages us to add knowledge to our faith in Jesus, and that is how we will know. Blind faith is just that—it is blind. It is a faith that has no vision or purpose or direction. Peter clearly wants us to have faith that can see Jesus and, through the transparency of Jesus, have a vision for God's kingdom. It requires solid thinking, fearless discernment, and a deep wisdom. When Jesus first stood before Peter on the shores of the Galilee, Peter knew something was up.

Feast your eyes on the painting of the calling of Peter and Andrew by the pre-Renaissance Italian artist Duccio. Several features will catch your attention. First, look at the hand of Jesus. It is open and it is inviting. Jesus has instructed Peter and Andrew to cast their nets where the fish are swimming just below the surface. We can see the fish. We can see Peter and Andrew pulling up the once-empty nets now loaded with fish. The fish clearly are not the most important matter in the painting. What is important is the open hand of Jesus and the interaction that is now taking place between the fishermen and Jesus.

Let your eyes gaze for a moment on Peter, who is dressed in a blue tunic. He is raising his hand. Is it a friendly gesture? Or is Peter raising his hand to question what Jesus is saying? We are not let in on the conversation. We know from the Gospel of Luke that Peter is saying to Jesus, "Go away from me, Lord, for I am a sinful man!" As we look at the painting by Duccio, we imagine the interaction between Peter and Jesus.

When he had finished speaking, he said to Simon, "Put out into the deep water and let down your nets for a catch." Simon answered, "Master, we have worked all night long but have caught nothing. Yet if you say so, I will let down the nets." When they had done this, they caught so many fish that their nets were beginning to break. So they signaled to their partners in the other boat to come and help them. And they came and filled both boats, so that they began to sink. But when Simon Peter saw it, he fell down at Jesus's knees, saying, "Go away from me, Lord, for I am a sinful man!"

Luke 5:4-8

Andrew is not passive. Jesus has caught his attention as well. The body language between Jesus and Andrew is also worth our consideration. Andrew appears attentive. It could be because he is interested in Jesus. It could also be because he is in a state of shock, bewilderment, and awe. This is one of those defining moments for Andrew. Life will never be the same. It is hard to get his head wrapped around the experience. It will take time to figure it all out. Again, as with Peter, the viewer is not let in on Andrew's verbal response. All we witness at this point of transition is his physical reaction.

Look at the colors in the painting and notice the golden background. Again, the mind is left to wonder if the golden sky is a sign of the revelation taking place—or is it simply the sun rising and the dawning of a new day? The point is that the artist wants us to think. He wants our attention. He doesn't want the details of his painting to slip by unnoticed. The postures, the gestures, the clothing, and the attention to emotion all play into the big picture that is before our eyes.

The Call

One of the more mysterious features of religious life is the call. When clergy talk about being "called" by God, there is a sense of being separated and being special. It is a label or a handle used to talk about one's reason for entering the ministry. People want to hear about the call almost as if they literally think God called the person on a telephone and there was an immediate connection.

The word *call* is really a little more down to earth. Derived from the Latin word *vocare* (to call), it is closely associated with a vocation, or it can be used to describe an avocation, something other than just a job. You name the profession, and behind it there is often a story of being called into a profession or a career to serve the greater good. A lawyer talks about a desire to bring justice, a doctor about a desire to heal, a teacher about a desire to educate, and so on.

The call is about what we and God are doing together. That is the nature of a vocation and a higher calling. The call has to do with an interaction or a dialogue of our deepest desire to do what God wants us to do. The call is in response to a desire, a yearning, a longing, and yes, a craving to be with God, to know God, and to do God's will.

> For this reason…we have not ceased praying for you and asking that you may be filled with the knowledge of God's will in all spiritual wisdom and understanding so that you may lead lives worthy of the Lord, fully pleasing to him, as you bear fruit in every good work and as you grow in the knowledge of God. (Colossians 1:9-10)

Without knowledge of God, the call can be reduced to simply discussing our desires and our yearnings. Without knowledge of the spiritual life, many modern-day professionals who followed their passions are left only with obsessions and compulsions and addictions. What started off as something good and sincere turned tragically into a nightmare as a result of our own sheer willpower and desire to take charge. Somewhere along the way, between vocation and profession and career, our primal desire to please God and to do God's will was captured and sabotaged, and self-centeredness took over. That may satisfy us for a while. In fact, whole careers can be built upon success, achievement, and rewards. But at the end of the day, the gold watch is not enough to satisfy our greatest desire for God and for doing God's will.

An Identity Change

The call is really a change in identity from living a self-centered life to leading one that is now centered in God's will being done on earth just as it is in heaven. Recall Peter was referred to as *bar-Jonah,* that is, the son of Jonah. Many of us are familiar with the story of Jonah and the whale, which is an early narrative that describes the power of God bringing life over death. For fishermen like Peter, there was probably no greater story than that of Jonah. Peter's identity in the name of Jonah was worthy of his profession. The story of Jonah is also a story of evangelism and witnessing to those in wicked Nineveh. However, it was because Jonah refused God's calling that he found himself tossed overboard during a storm. Now it is Peter's turn.

Jesus calls Peter to leave the water. Jesus calls Peter to give up fishing and instead fish for lost souls. Jesus calls Peter to step out of the known into the unknown. Jesus also calls Peter to live with God and to "seek first God's kingdom" (Matthew 6:33). "Follow me," Jesus says. It is, for Peter, like being tossed overboard.

To this invitation, and to this higher calling, Peter cries out, "Go away from me, Lord, for I am a sinful man!" (Luke 5:8). Although this outwardly appears as rejection on Peter's part, inwardly it is the cry of everyman who does not feel worthy and who does not feel capable of doing God's will. It is too much to ask. "Yes," on one hand, we desire God; but "no," on the other hand, we tell ourselves it is too difficult and too tall of an order. Here, in this paradox in which we struggle, Jesus extends the hand of grace and says to Peter and to all who follow him, "Do not be afraid" (Luke 5:10).

Grace gives us the strength to do what we are normally not capable of doing on our own. Grace provides us with a second chance. And so Peter and Andrew brought their boats to shore, and they left everything and followed Jesus. By grace, Peter accepted the call. Now, by grace, Peter will learn about a new life and he will gain knowledge of the kingdom of God and he will grow spiritually. Peter knew all about fishing. What he didn't know was how he was supposed to fish for people. Grace would help Peter catch hold of God at work in his life. Grace would help Peter cast a vision for his life that would be deeper than dropping a net in the sea. Grace gave Peter the power to think in a new way. There is power in knowledge.

Growth Point—Knowledge

In leaving everything, Peter now had space to think. Images and ideas and thoughts are all important as we develop knowledge that provides structure to the way in which we think about our spiritual lives and our desire to be with God. Thinking and specifically knowing about truth adds to and supports our primary desire. We know right from wrong. We know what is good from bad. We know what is true and what is false. How do we know? Faith informed by the power of grace helps us to know.

The word *agnostic* literally means to not know. Many people profess to be agnostic. There is a danger in not knowing. It leaves us vulnerable to ignorance. Stinking-thinking, trying to draw straight lines with crooked pencils and ignoring the information that informs and shapes our minds, can stunt our spiritual growth. Rather than honor and love God with all of our minds, we dishonor God by having no knowledge of him and by not thinking about our faith. Peter writes, "add knowledge with goodness" (2 Peter 1:5). Knowledge provides us with an understanding of truth, and as a result we are given direction and purpose and meaning.

Duccio paints life in the boat as small and limited. The mind and knowledge can be that way as well. The call by Jesus expands our thinking and encourages us to go deeper. Saint Paul writes about this bigger picture as follows:

> Whatever is true, whatever is honorable, whatever is just, whatever is pure, whatever is pleasing, whatever is commendable, if there is any excellence and if there is anything worthy of praise, think about these things. (Philippians 4:8)

Knowledge is more than information about interesting facts and figures and formulas. It is not about being a know-it-all. It is about truth. There is power in knowledge, but only when the knowledge is true.

Knowledge that is added to goodness is about interacting with the truth. In other words, knowledge or knowing in the biblical sense was always understood as something more than head knowledge or simply the intellect. Knowledge or knowing has to do with interacting with God in an intimate way. When God knows what is in our hearts, it is a way of describing this intimate relationship. When we talk of knowing what God wants for our lives, we are inspired or filled with God's spirit. This is an intimate knowledge that feeds our souls.

Knowledge of this sort is different from the kind of knowledge we are often given in our culture. Knowledge of faith is not anti-intellectual. Rather, it is a knowledge that cares for the soul. Without this knowledge, the soul would be impoverished.

The Bible shows us that there are some people who are too smart for their own good. The Bible is filled with examples of some of the smartest people who do some of the dumbest things. Clearly, it is the Bible that warns us, "Pride comes before the fall" (Proverbs 16:18). Knowledge of God is humbling. It is in humility we are given the spiritual knowledge that we are not God. It is in humility we discover God's power.

The call extended to Peter and Andrew is an invitation to come and follow Jesus and to know and to interact with Jesus about the truth of God and God's desire to save a broken world. Yes, catching fish is important. But by extending the call, Jesus makes Peter and Andrew aware that by catching hold of the truth and by reeling in the knowledge of their greatest desire to live with God, they will discover what is even more important. In fact, Jesus says, "I am the way and the truth and the life" (John 14:6). Imagine being in that little boat with Peter and Andrew as Jesus stands before them and calls them to the truth found not in a boat but in the larger knowledge of greater life that can be found in God's kingdom.

Again, this is a matter of faith. Sure, Peter and Andrew had faith in fishing. But that night they caught nothing, and they had run out of energy. They were depleted. The next day, Jesus had them cast their nets on the other side of the boat. It was time to cast their nets in a new direction. It was time to go deeper. It was time to catch hold of their greatest desire.

Kingdom Life

Here is what we know: "God so loved the world that he gave his only Son, so that everyone who believes in him may not perish but they may have eternal life" (John 3:16). Often we think of eternal life as something that happens to us after we die. As Peter and Andrew and the disciples began to follow Jesus, they discovered that eternal life has to do with participating in God's divine nature and living with God right now.

The question is not "Is there life after death?" The better question becomes "Is there life after birth?" Recall this in the conversation Jesus had with Nicodemus about being born from above (John 3:1-21). A second birth or being born again is a way of describing not our natural birth but a spiritual birth that opens us to a "life that is really life" (I Timothy 6:19). What we find in eternal life is life with God that is available to us right now through Jesus. It is abundant life not because it is filled with material things, but it is abundant because it is filled with God.

Abundant life, eternal life, life with God is Kingdom life. As the disciples walked and talked with Jesus, it was apparent that their knowledge of this Kingdom life added to their faith in Jesus. They received the vision of the Kingdom from their trust in Jesus, and now they were beginning to see the reality of this vision through their knowledge. Their knowledge came as they placed their confidence (*con-fidere:* to have faith with) in Jesus. They relied on Jesus. They found Jesus to be a reliable source of information whose ideas and thoughts and images shaped their knowledge. It was a deep, personal knowledge. They knew that their faith had caught hold of the truth.

They also knew that faith takes a great deal of work. Faith requires effort on our parts. Again, this is where knowledge helps and adds to our faith. It is easy to become lazy and take faith for granted. Knowledge keeps us sharp. Knowledge defends our faith: "May the peace of God, which surpasses all understanding, guard your hearts and minds in the *knowledge* and love of God and our Lord Jesus Christ…" (Philippians 4:7). Knowledge helps us see the vision of the Kingdom life at work in our life right now. Knowledge at this level is very personal.

Stepping Stone—Prayer

The most intimate form of communication we have with God is prayer. The way in which we get to know Jesus is by talking with him, praying to him, reflecting upon his word that is written in scripture, and praying about how that word speaks to us. There are many times the disciples watched and observed Jesus in prayer, and they learned from him. They knew prayer was important. They would learn why it was important as they walked and talked and followed Jesus in his earthly ministry.

No greater learning came for Peter than when the disciples followed Jesus into Jerusalem before the Crucifixion. Peter knew by this time that prayer for Jesus was not a last resort but a first resource that equipped Jesus and God to work together. Prayer preceded whatever Jesus did. Jesus prayed first then acted. Jesus had taught the disciples how to pray and he had taught them about the perseverance of prayer. He said to them, "Ask and it will be given to you; search and you will find it; knock and the door will be opened" (Luke 11:10). Now, as they made their way up into the Upper Room where they prepared the Passover feast and the Last Supper, Jesus turned to Peter and said, "Simon, Simon, listen! Satan has demanded to sift all of you like wheat, but I have prayed for you that your own faith may not fail; and once you have turned back, strengthen your brothers" (Luke 22:31-32).

"Simon," Jesus says, referring to Peter before the call. The name Simon reminded Peter of life before he stood on the rock. The name Simon was a human identity of mortal nature. Peter was headed into the test and trial of his life. He was about to face Satan. Jesus made it clear that Satan would sift Peter like wheat. The image was gruesome. Peter would be picked to pieces, broken apart and crushed.

But Jesus prays for Peter. When we pray, we place our lives in God's control. When we pray, we figure out what we are going to do with God. When we pray, we interact and participate in the divine nature of God's kingdom. Jesus prayed. Peter did not. Peter ignored prayer. When we ignore something, we become ignorant. So Peter spoke only with self-confidence: "Lord, I am ready to go with you to prison and death" (Luke 22:33). Peter lacked knowledge.

Jesus said, "I tell you, Peter, the cock will not crow this day until you deny three times that you know me" (Luke 22:34). As Peter faces the trial with Satan, there is no mention of prayer. Is it any surprise scripture records three times Peter saying "I do not know the man?" Prayer reveals knowledge.

Through the growth point of prayer, we add knowledge of God to our faith. With the knowledge of God interacting in our lives, we increase our faith, and our vision for spiritual growth expands through self-control.

May You Live in Christ!

For Reflection and Discussion

GROWTH POINT—Knowledge
If a picture is worth a thousand words, what are some of the words that come to your mind when you look at the pre-Renaissance painting by the artist Duccio?
--what might the conversation be like between Jesus and the disciples?
--can you imagine putting into your own words the calling of Peter and Andrew?
--is a calling something that is known? Did you ever know a calling?
--as a result of the call, what did you know? Would life be different?

As you gaze further into the painting, what do you make of the fish? Do the fish represent the unknown? Or are the fish a symbol of what will be known?
--what is the role of faith as you spiritually grow in the knowledge of God?
--for you, does knowledge inform faith or does faith inform knowledge?
--biblical knowledge is an intimate interaction. How is that different from our understanding and the way we often use the word *knowledge*?
--how has knowledge of God assisted you in spiritual growth and change?

STEPPING STONE—Prayer
In what ways has prayer helped form and shape your knowledge of God?
--do you pray on a regular basis? Can you describe your prayer life?
--where do you pray? How do you pray? Why do you pray?
--do you keep a prayer journal? Do you notice themes or spiritual issues?
--has that practice helped with your spiritual knowledge of God? How so?

What might help you think of prayer not as a last resort but as a first resource?
--has prayer been for you a matter of asking and getting or is it about knowing?
--what would happen if, instead of you doing all the talking, you sat in silence?
--what might God say? How would you know it was God speaking to you?
--have you ever sought spiritual guidance? Why? Why not?

6
Self-Control

Add to knowledge self-control
(2 Peter 1:6)

"Add to knowledge self-control," Peter writes. Notice self-control comes after our knowledge of God and after we have placed our lives under the control of God. Only when God is in control of our lives do we find inner control—the ability to be self-governed, managed, ruled, and accountable in ways that are now in accordance with God's will and purposes. Only when we first report to God do we find the inner self moving away from a self-centered existence to a more centered self that is under a higher authority—the lordship of Jesus Christ. Peter obviously learned this understanding of self-control the hard way—perhaps in the most heartbreaking way imaginable. Unfortunately, it is the human way.

Look at Rembrandt's famous painting. The spotlight is again on Peter. The light is on him. Light is of God. Light often represents glory. Christ is the light of the world. But this is one of the darkest hours. Why the light?

Light has the ability to reveal. It reveals the face of Peter. At first blush, he looks innocent. He looks open. He looks trustworthy. Of course, all we are looking at is his outward appearance, and we know that "men look on the outward appearance, but the Lord looks on the heart" (I Samuel 16:7).

There, beside the flicker of the fire, the servant girl looks closely at him. She looks into his eyes. It is a way of looking into his soul. She listens to his voice and his accent. As a servant girl, she anticipates the needs of others. She is ready to help. She has been trained to serve.

Then they seized him and led him away, bringing him into the high priest's house. But Peter was following at a distance. When they had kindled a fire in the middle of the courtyard and sat down together, Peter sat among them. Then a servant-girl, seeing him in the firelight, stared at him and said, "This man also was with him." But he denied it, saying, "Woman, I do not know him." A little later someone else, on seeing him, said, "You also are one of them." But Peter said, "Man, I am not!" Then about an hour later, yet another kept insisting, "Surely this man also was with him; for he is a Galilean." But Peter said, "Man, I do not know what you are talking about!" At that moment, while he was still speaking, the cock crowed. The Lord turned and looked at Peter. Then Peter remembered the word of the Lord, how he had said to him, "Before the cock crows today, you will deny me three times." And he went out and wept bitterly.

Luke 22:54-62

Even at her age, she understands her position. She is capable. She looks closely at Peter and something does not add up.

Peter has had a terrible day, and more often than not we respond by retreating and escaping into a world we think we can control. We think we are in self-control. The reality is we are wildly out of control.

"This man was with him," the servant girl tells the crowd in the courtyard during one of Jesus's trials. But Peter denies it. Wouldn't you? Isn't there a part of all of us that is sometimes fearful of telling the truth? Are we willing to sacrifice our security just for the truth? We all can identify with the conflicted emotions and inner turmoil Peter was going through. After all, the Roman soldiers are there beside the flickering of the flame. Their presence alone would silence most people. And so the Gospel peels apart the layers of Peter's psyche—and more importantly his soul—one denial upon another.

It is easy to scoff at Peter. Peter is human. And it is not just Peter who denies reality, who denies the truth, much less who denies Jesus. We are all standing in the shadow of the flickering light with Peter. And so Peter denies Jesus once, twice, three times, and we hear the crow of the rooster. As Peter was denying his relationship to Jesus, he may have appeared to the people in the courtyard to be a man under self-control. But his appearance is deceiving. Peter is under the control of deception, darkness, and denial. He is out of control.

When we believe we are in control, then we believe we can influence or determine the outcome. Not only that—when we believe we are in control, then we believe we are responsible for the outcome as well.

I can remember one Friday morning being in the Dallas/Fort Worth airport. I was scheduled to fly back home to Louisville for a wedding rehearsal Friday evening and a wedding on Saturday. You can already predict what happened. I was sitting there, waiting to board, when I looked at the monitor listing the flight schedules. One flight after another, the sign flashed "delayed." My plane, however, had not been listed, and so I felt somehow immune. It didn't take long, however, before the "delayed" sign went up. Inside, I was in turmoil. I spoke to an agent and explained my situation, which at the time sounded so unique and pressing. The reality was everyone had a story to tell and mine was only one of many. I was told there was bad weather in the west and storms in the east and lightning all around and it was creating havoc in major airports all around the country. Sure enough, within minutes the "cancelled" sign flashed beside my flight, and I about went ballistic. Eventually I was able to reach my associate, and all was well. Still, it remains a good example in my life of how strange it gets when we lose control.

Come back with me to Peter and the little servant girl who intimidated him. She simply recognized and identified Peter. That was all. She was a little servant girl. Peter was a big man. You can see the difference in their sizes as portrayed in Rembrandt's painting. But this little servant girl intimidated Peter. It was not exactly a federal case. It was simply the truth. She simply told the truth, and Peter countered her truth with a lie. Don't ever forget who is the father of lies—the devil.

According to the Gospel, Peter was next identified by a bystander. Then a third time he was recognized and called out. "At that moment, as he was still speaking, the cock crowed. The Lord turned and looked at Peter." One can only imagine the humiliation. Jesus looked at Peter. Jesus knew the devil was "sifting Peter like wheat" (Luke 22:31). Peter, who had wanted to be in control, left the courtyard and wept bitterly. His life was now out of control.

The Dark Night of the Soul

The dark night of the soul is a technical term used first by the sixteenth-century mystic St. John of the Cross to describe the collapse of the inner self. In modern times, this phrase of a "dark night" has been reduced to having a bad day or losing a job or some kind of conflict that makes it hard to sleep for a night or two. Some have used the label of a "dark night of the soul" to describe depression. Others have been intrigued by the term and have been drawn to it as something to experience.

For the sake of our discussion on spiritual growth, the dark night is an intensely spiritual matter that may include all of the above, but be reminded of Peter and what was going on with his denial. His dark night was not a relational problem or a psychological matter but more a matter for the soul.

The soul houses our prayer lives. The soul covers and contains our identities. More importantly, it is the soul that generates our understanding of God. The soul reveals the way we appear before God. It is not the responsibility of the soul to put our best feet forward before God. The soul simply and profoundly presents us before God. It is here in the soul that we begin to imagine our lives before God, and it is in the soul God enters and creates new lives for us. Unfortunately, it is here in the soul many of us build our walls to shut God out and deny God access and sadly lose God's presence in our lives. It is here Peter employs his will to override the soul and to go it alone.

It is, however, the soul that organizes our lives around God, so when we harm and injure, our souls—life with God—obviously become broken and disorganized.

Peter denies Jesus three times. In so doing, Peter collapses mentally, physically, and spiritually. Peter has followed Jesus and has done much of what Jesus has asked, except for losing his life in order to find it, and except for denying himself and picking up his cross, and except for placing his life under the control of God's will. This is what self-control is all about. It is about placing our lives under God's control and allowing God to govern our runaway egos. In order to find self-control, Peter needed first to turn his life over to the God of greater control.

As he stands by the flickering charcoal flame, we see in Peter a broken man who has created Jesus in his own image. This assessment may seem harsh or it may seem overly simplistic, but what the dark night of the soul teaches us is that, first of all, the way in which we perceive God is often inadequate. As J. B. Phillips wrote in his classic *Your God Is Too Small*, we are reminded that our relationships with God are too-often one sided and cozy and based only on our needs and our wants, which do little to place our selves under the Lord's control.

Again, it is easy for us on this side of the Resurrection to have the sense that God will prove victorious and Jesus will rise from the dead and evil will be conquered and every tear will be wiped away, but try telling this to someone who is going through the darkness. Tell this to someone whose life is out of control.

May I suggest, rather than looking at the dark night as yet another "phase" we might be going through or yet another "learning experience," let's open our eyes to this utter darkness as an important movement within the soul whereby we embrace the essence of our beings. The dark night is not encountered as some kind of rung on the spiritual ladder that we have climbed, but see it more through Peter's eyes: it is a total loss of the way Peter imagined God and the way Peter imagined himself.

Again, without dwelling on the dark night and using merely a psychological explanation to describe what has occurred in the life of Peter, it is important to raise the question of evil in the darkness. *Diabolis,* the Spanish reference to the devil, is best defined as "that which breaks apart." The devil is known for being destructive. In fact, the devil is unable to create—only destroy. *Symbolis* is the Spanish derivative for "symbol," and it best describes "that which pulls together."

Growth Point—Self-Control

One of the most important dynamics of the dark night of the soul, and certainly it is embedded within our very souls, is when we hear and actually begin to understand the words of Jesus, who says that "whoever loses their life for my sake will find it" (Matthew 10:39).

Although some people may at first blush read this as a negative message, the point Jesus is making is pretty clear and direct and quite positive. There is hope. There is a promise. There is a future. There is life with God. You will find it.

That is the message for all who have experienced or are going through the dark night. This is not something trite like "when one door closes, another will open." It is a rough and tough understanding of life.

The positive nature of losing our lives is found in the understanding that we will find life—with God. We lose a life that is self-centered—where those walls have been built all around the self over the years—only to find, in the dark night, the walls come tumbling down and a new self that is centered in God emerges. It is a centered self. Recall the words from Psalm 139:

> If I say "surely the darkness shall cover me,
> and the light around me become night,"
> even the darkness is not dark to you;
> the night is as bright as the day,
> for darkness is as light to you.
> For it was you who formed my inward parts;
> you knit me together in my mother's womb.
>
> (vss. 11-13)

God is the creator. No longer are we the point of reference for life. This is a hard lesson, a difficult truth for anyone to learn. For Peter, it was an eye opener. It was the beginning of a new vision for life. He would be under God's control. Being under God's control means that God is the reference point, the center point, and that point is made clear to Peter as he watches Jesus pick up his Cross. With his focus entirely on Jesus, Peter begins to find a new self that is under control and governed by his Lord.

How Many Times Must I Forgive?

As Peter watched Jesus being beaten and mocked by the soldiers, his heart was no doubt broken. So too were his mind and his soul. But it is here that Jesus and the Cross do their amazing work, not only on Peter but on all who follow Jesus.

"Love the Lord your God with all your heart and all your soul and all your mind." You know that is the first and greatest commandment. And the second is like unto it: "Love your neighbor as yourself." We say that commandment and some of us have memorized it and we reflect on it periodically. But now, as Jesus carries his Cross to Golgotha, the place of the skull, is that really the first thought and the first commandment that come to your mind?

As Peter watched his Lord, who knows what crossed his mind. What we do know is Peter's mind was rubbed raw and depleted and exhausted from his denials and from his dying to self. If anything, his mind was more like a blank slate—a tabula rasa—that was waiting to be written upon or to be impressed upon. The mind sometimes is thus in the transition where we are waiting for the future while living in the uncertainty of the present and holding only to the experience of the past.

So if Peter went back into his past, he would have remembered an earlier question he had for Jesus: "Lord, if another member of the church sins against me, how often should I forgive? As many as seven times?" Jesus said to him, "Not seven times, but, I tell you, seventy times seven."

Just as Jesus said "seventy times seven," Peter no doubt began to calculate in his mind the correct number. He knew seventy times seven was a lot. Like most people, when Peter heard Jesus's response, he began to grasp for a number based on some kind of mathematical equation. The truth of the matter is Jesus is not trying to stump us with an equation; he is opening our minds to think about the Kingdom. Kingdom life is about forgiveness. One way of dying to ourselves and rising to a new self is to learn how to forgive. When we live in the Kingdom, when we place our selves under the Lord, and when God rules, we forgive.

To expand and advance our understanding of forgiveness, Jesus reinforces his teaching to Peter and to the disciples and to all who have ears to hear that "the kingdom of heaven may be compared to a king who wished to settle his accounts with his slaves" (Matthew 18:23). One slave fell to his knees and begged forgiveness. The king, out of pity for the slave, forgave him of his debt.

That same slave, however, found a fellow slave who owed him money, and he refused to forgive him and actually tossed him in prison until he could pay his debt. The king was outraged. And in his anger, his lord handed him over to be tortured until he would pay his entire debt. So it will be, Jesus says, "If you do not forgive your brother or sister from your heart" (Matthew 18:35).

The operative word in this parable is *forgiveness*. Forgiveness is a Kingdom value. We find forgiveness in the Kingdom. There is an infinite amount of forgiveness in God's kingdom. To not forgive sets us outside the Kingdom. It is that simple.

The parable was etched in Peter's mind. After his denials, Peter was tortured with guilt, remorse, shame, and the darkness that had enveloped him. As he had stood next to the warmth of the charcoal fire, his heart had remained cold, and before the little servant girl, he had denied Jesus. Peter needed to be forgiven. Peter knew forgiveness was not about a number like seven times seven that could somehow be figured out. Forgiveness has to do with grace, and it is a Kingdom value and it is beyond our calculations. Surely at the Cross, Peter began to figure this out in his mind and in his heart and in his soul.

Stepping Stone—Forgiveness

Forgiveness is the stepping stone to a life under God's control. Here is why: we are told in scripture, "We love because God has first loved us" (I John 4:19). I think it fair to say we also forgive because God has first forgiven us. Until we first accept God's forgiveness, it is hard, if not impossible, to forgive others. Put another way, until we first accept God's love for us, it is hard, if not impossible, to love others. Forgiveness and love go together. The two are inextricably bound.

At the Cross, Peter saw with his own eyes the love of Jesus poured out like blood. Blood often was interpreted in scripture as life. When Peter saw the blood of Jesus poured out for him on the Cross, he saw with his own eyes life-with-God being poured out for him. This life was filled with love. "God so loved the world that he gave his only begotten Son so that whoever believes in him may not perish but have everlasting life" (John 3:16).

Oh, it is so easy not to forgive. The easier act is to hold onto resentments and hurts and betrayals. The problem with not forgiving is that it keeps us locked in the past where we have been hurt. It is easy not to forgive, but it is not good for the soul. It is also not easy to accept forgiveness, but again, not to accept forgiveness strains the way we live and interact with others.

As Peter stood before the Cross, he heard the words "Father, forgive them," and they penetrated his very being. By accepting his Lord's forgiveness, there at the Cross, Peter would find a life of self-control as he "looked to Jesus the pioneer and perfector of our faith, who for the sake of the joy that was set before him endured the Cross…" Watch now, as endurance will help us see more clearly life under the self-control of the Lord.

Rev. Robert T. Jennings

For Reflection and Discussion

GROWTH POINT—Self-control

Look at the Rembrandt painting and the spotlight on Peter. He is doing everything he possibly can to look in control on the outside. What might his inner world be like?

--if you were a disciple, what advice might you have given Peter at this point?
--have you ever been in a position before of denial or shading the truth?
--what do you make of the shades and colors Rembrandt chooses?
--what do you know about the experience of being totally out of control?

Self-control is found when the self is placed under the control of the Lord. It is not about controlling ourselves. It is about turning ourselves over to the Lord's control.

--have you had the experience of being under the Lord's control? Elaborate.
--what did the Lord do to place you under control? Show mercy? Forgive?
--when you were under control, did the Lord provide you with a new way to live?
--did you find your "self" then under control? Why is that? What did you learn?

STEPPING STONE—Forgiveness

Recall when Peter asked the question, "Lord, how often should I forgive?" The question comes back to Peter as he denies his Lord. How many times should Peter forgive?

--Kingdom living is about forgiving. It is not calculating. How can that be?
--have you found forgiveness to be a Kingdom value? Why is that so?
--is a Kingdom value worth more than something of value in our world? Why?
--why does Jesus say "lay up treasures in heaven"? Name some treasures.

May You Live in Christ!

Forgiveness is a stepping stone to placing our lives under God's control. What do you know about forgiveness in your life? Have you ever forgiven another?
   --have you ever been forgiven? Can you recall what that was like?
   --have you ever experienced God's forgiveness? When?
    How do you know?
   --what about forgiving yourself? What do you know about that?
   --why do you think confession is good for the soul?

7
Endurance

Make every effort to add to your faith...endurance
(2 Peter 1:6)

Suffering is awful. I hate to suffer. Like many people, I do everything within reason to avoid pain. I wouldn't consider myself a "baby," but let's just say when I see suffering coming my way, I duck. When I see someone I love suffer, it hurts all the more.

There is emotional suffering. There is physical suffering. There is spiritual suffering. And there is more. Remember Peter who had denied Jesus three times and then at the Cross experienced forgiveness? There is sacrificial suffering. Jesus makes suffering sacred.

We are not going to get out of this world without suffering. How we suffer, therefore, is a choice we all must make. Jesus and the disciples had left the Sea of Galilee, and behind them they had left not only their fishing but also their old ideas, beliefs, thoughts, and ways they viewed life. For example, as soon as they had accepted the call to follow Jesus, the disciples encountered a leper who was sitting on the outskirts of the city.

Take a moment and look at the painting by Frank Wesley. The disciples are standing back, looking at the leper. Leprosy is highly contagious. The disciples are keeping a safe distance. Often what we try to do when we encounter suffering is step back and remove ourselves from the scene. The disciples, who only days earlier had accepted the call to follow Jesus, were now hesitant. No doubt they were wondering, "Is this what following Jesus is about?" As you gaze at the picture, you can almost hear the questions and the reservations surface in the disciples' minds.

Once, when he was in one of the cities, there was a man covered with leprosy. When he saw Jesus, he bowed with his face to the ground and begged him, "Lord, if you choose, you can make me clean." Then Jesus stretched out his hand, touched him, and said, "I do choose. Be made clean." Immediately the leprosy left him. And he ordered him to tell no one. "Go," he said, "and show yourself to the priest, and, as Moses commanded, make an offering for your cleansing, for a testimony to them." But now more than ever the word about Jesus spread abroad; many crowds would gather to hear him and to be cured of their diseases. But he would withdraw to deserted places and pray.

Luke 5:12-16

Yet Jesus changes our perspective on suffering with one swift move. Look at Jesus as he bends over and, at eye level, not only looks the leper in the face but also looks suffering and death in the face. Death is often knocking on the doorstep of leprosy. That is what makes leprosy so frightening. Death is just around the corner. What does the leper do until death? That is not the question. The better question is, "How can the leper find life?"

It is by embracing this question the leper is overheard saying to Jesus, "Lord, if you choose, you can make me clean." By his making this request, it is apparent the leper has chosen life—he is on the side of life. As we look at the painting, we see the vulture, who, as the symbol of death, now prepares to fly away. "Lord, if you choose"—if you choose to enter the arena of suffering—now that is a potent request.

Healing

I have spent a large part of my ministry involved in the dynamic of healing. Many people are put off at the mere mention of healing. For some, spiritual healing sounds fake or manipulative. The list of objections is endless. I think I have heard them all. When I approach healing, I keep this little story of the healing of the leper in mind. It is a paradigm for healing. It is a reminder from the Gospel of Luke (the dear and glorious physician) that this encounter with the leper is a first example, a first impression that Peter and the disciples experienced while watching Jesus in action. First impressions are lasting, and that is one reason this story is important.

What the disciples experienced was healing in the midst of suffering. Again, what I have experienced over the years is a deep and abiding appreciation for the power of healing that continues through the witness of the church. Healing takes many forms. Sure, there is physical healing and the healing of the body. There is also emotional healing, which heals everything from toxic emotions to terrible thoughts to memories from the past and dread for the future.

Relational healing is as important as the healing of the mind and body. The healing of relationships, often through forgiveness and mercy, is an antidote for so much suffering we see on a daily basis.

I would be remiss if I didn't draw attention to the importance of spiritual healing. I worked as a spiritual director and helped people with their prayers, the working of the Holy Spirit in their lives, and ultimately their distorted images of God, which for whatever reason were in need of healing. What was often discovered—for some, for the first time—was a God who cares. They learned of the God who enters their suffering. Not only that, there was in this understanding of God a new sense of triumph and courage in the midst of suffering that "if God is for us, who can be against us?" (Romans 8:31). Such a discovery paves the way for the growth point of endurance.

The ultimate form of healing is found in discovering life-with-God. This is eternal life. It is abundant life. Remember, it is zoe life. It is "taking hold of life that really is life" (I Timothy 6:19). This is life in Christ, and it is what Peter saw from his first day in following Jesus, to the empty tomb, to his first-century worship in the space now far beneath the Vatican, to his life when it was no longer present on earth. *Vivatis in Christo!* This is the cry of healing that Peter makes known to us through his vision of Jesus as Lord of life and through the spiritual growth that occurs when we see this vision at work.

Suffering and Life

I'll never forget visiting a household where an elderly woman had just died after a heart attack. The final years of her life had been terribly difficult as a result of a series of strokes. She was incapacitated in almost all aspects of her life. When I was greeted at the door by the husband, who was not active in the church, I made the mistake of saying something like "what a blessing" she finally was no longer in pain. The husband looked at me with steely eyes and said, "You will never know how long she suffered; there was no blessing about it."

After we talked a little bit about the funeral arrangements, he stood up, and it became clear to me that it was time to leave. As I made my way to the door, I tried to think of something consoling to say, and I blurted out, "Her suffering reminds us of how Jesus suffered on the Cross." The husband again looked at me as a young know-it-all clergyman—this time almost with pity as to how pitiful I was—and he said, "Are you kidding me? Jesus suffered for a day. My wife suffered for five years. There is no comparison." I left lost for words.

Being lost for words is not always a bad thing. Sometimes, when we are lost for words, it allows God the opportunity to speak. Something I heard from God that day was "comparisons are odious." I learned to keep my comparisons to myself. I also learned not to compare Jesus and his suffering to that of anyone else. Suffering is unique. So too is life. What I began to learn that day when I stumbled all over myself is not that much different from what Peter and the disciples learned from Jesus and the leper: suffering and life go together.

It is hard to live and not suffer. The two—suffering and life—seem inextricably bound. Suffering is simply a part of life. It has a way of showing up.

Some probably thought the leper deserved his disease and somehow deserved suffering. Be careful when deciding who deserves what. I think this is one of the reasons why Jesus went quickly, like a blowtorch, into that place of indignation with the Pharisees time and time again, because so often they calculated who was deserving and who was not.

The beatitudes in the Sermon on the Mount are such a radically different way of approaching life and suffering. Jesus says:

Blessed are the poor in spirit, for theirs is the kingdom of heaven.
Blessed are those who mourn, for they will be comforted.
Blessed are the meek, for they will inherit the earth. (Matthew 5:3-5)

The list continues. What is apparent is that Jesus identifies those who have been brought to the place where they can no longer rely on their own strength but must rely on the power of God.

Growth Point—Endurance

Peter identifies the gift of endurance as one of the ways we can see through suffering, pain, and heartache without losing our faith. Often, when we mention the word *endurance*, people put their heads down. It sounds so negative. It sounds as if we are that kitten seen on the poster holding onto a tree limb with the caption "Hang in there." *Endurance* sounds like we are simply hanging in there.

May I suggest, after the disciples' encounter with the leper, they saw and had a vision of so much more. *Endurance* is a proactive word. How long the leper had been sitting beside the tree on the outskirts of the city—God only knows. What we do know is that in the midst of his suffering, the leper called out to Jesus with the words "Lord, if you choose," then don't walk by, don't stare at me, but enter my suffering. Those of us who have suffered know that when God is with us, we move from a place of being "poor in spirit" and simply at a loss to now being able to endure, thanks to the strength of grace. With endurance, fueled by grace, we discover meaning, purpose, and value. Suffering does not get the last word.

A transition occurs. So often when we suffer, we choose to be alone, to complain, to cry out and to shake our fists at the sky above and to protect what is left in our lives to the very last breath. In actuality, such a response diminishes what is left of our lives and what remains of our souls. By choosing to allow God into the place of our hurt and loss, we find that it expands our vision, develops our character, and helps us grow spiritually. This is not about simply putting on a happy face or putting lipstick on that pig of suffering. It is about discovering a gift in the midst of our turmoil and heartache. It is about recognizing, seeing, and opening our eyes to a new reality.

As a clergyman for more than forty years, I have seen untold heartache. Many of the stories are not mine to tell. My wife and I have personally lived through some very difficult times with our four grown sons. One son almost lost his daughter to a strange virus, another went through four tours in Iraq as a Marine helicopter pilot, and another currently suffers from stage-four cancer. Trust me, we have been hurt deeply, but again these are not my stories to tell.

I can write about my brother, who committed suicide when I was in my first year of seminary. As a young seminarian, I can remember the terrible isolation and the feeling like I had done something wrong or it was my fault or there was something crazy about me when word got out that my brother had killed himself. Of course, no one knew my brother at seminary, nor did they know anything about his situation, and so basically all they could do was either look at me with pity or look away with avoidance.

The former dean of the seminary did approach me one day. He said to me, "I would like to talk with you. You and I have something in common." Naturally, I was thinking, "Like what?" After a few dark weeks, I did manage to set up a time to meet with him. My wife and I went over to his house. I was nervous. He showed me a picture of his son, a high school football star, who in his first year of college committed suicide. There was an immediate bond. There was a relief and a sense of peace I will never forget. I was not alone in suffering.

We talked for hours that night, and then over the remaining years in seminary we continued to meet for coffee, and I managed to take several elective classes under his teaching. However, what I learned from him most of all was his desire to endure. Sure, he carried the pain of his son's suicide around with him wherever he went, as I still carry the pain of my brother's. There will always be holes in our hearts. In fact, as I write, my heart is still as tender in this spot as the day my brother died. But life goes forward and the question, as always, is whether we will go forward into the future or stay stuck in the past and defined by our hurt. The choice is always before us. The choice to ask God into our suffering is the growing edge and beginning of endurance.

I have often preached that if you want to know where God is, just go to the end of your rope, and you will find him. It is not a joke. It is true.

And I learned this truth in seminary, there at the end of my rope. It was not like God came to me in a thunderous voice or with a sudden clap of thunder, but God did come to me as a choice. Like with Joshua, the point was brought home to me to "choose this day whom you will serve" (Joshua 24:15). It was not an easy choice.

Like the leper, I sat there in my grief, and I said in effect, "Lord, if you choose, you can make me clean" (Luke 5:12). Well, the Lord did not exactly me make me clean or make all the grief in my life disappear, but he did enter my world.

Yes, it is Jesus who "endured the Cross, disregarding its shame" (Hebrews 12:2), and I also heard loud and clear that "love bears all things, believes all things, hopes all things and…*endures* all things" (I Corinthians 13:7). There I sat, profoundly aware that if I left seminary, which I was so tempted to do, that would be yet another loss. Denying God would be a form of self-destruction.

Walking away from the fact that Jesus did choose to make me clean would be arrogant. The Lord opened my eyes to the choice I needed now to make. I could continue in a downward spiral, or I could endure. The choice was clearly mine to make.

Stepping Stone—Patience

By grace, I chose the path of endurance, and now, forty years later, I look back at that time as if it were yesterday. It wasn't just a close call as much as it was a time when I received a second calling. I was saved by endurance. Jesus says, "By your endurance, you will gain your souls" (Luke 21:19). One of the reasons I think we gain our souls is that through the gift and vision of endurance, we not only receive meaning and purpose and value, but we also find with endurance a growing commitment through the power of patience.

So many people are impatient, stressed, anxious, and looking for an instant fix. That is not the way of endurance. Rather, endurance teaches us first and foremost to commit ourselves to God and to people in all walks of life and also to make a commitment to ourselves. It is out of this commitment we are given the gift of patience. One of the things I learned early on with my struggle over losing my brother was that life was no longer the same for me. I was going to have to learn to live without him. So I made a commitment to God, and I was ordained. My commitment to my wife was solid and growing as our children were born. Making a commitment to endure moves us from being stuck in the past. While still honoring the past, by endurance we move patiently into the present and open to where God may be leading us into the future. It is all thanks to endurance.

To say I am a work in progress is a mild understatement, but it is apparent that with endurance comes patience. Patience allows Christ to be revealed and for Christ to enter our lives even during some of the most difficult and stressful times. Patience brings us to a point where we are not so much in a hurry, as we are now able to trust the Lord who is at work in us and "cleaning" us, or healing us, so that we may live in him and he in us. Patience leads us from the place of endurance to a growing life in Christ, where we now live the vision through a life of godliness.

May You Live in Christ!

For Reflection and Discussion

GROWTH POINT—Endurance

Endurance is born out of suffering. In order to grow in endurance, we must first choose how we respond to suffering. Do we invite God into our suffering or do we go it alone?

- --look at the painting by Frank Wesley. He pictures Jesus bent over, holding hands with the leper. The disciples stand back. What is your reaction?
- --what do you think was going on with the leper when he called out to Jesus?
- --why might Jesus have stopped, held hands, and focused on the leper?
- --imagine what the disciples were thinking and saying to one another.
- --how does this painting help you picture the place of endurance in your life?

Endurance provides us with a way not of getting around suffering but of getting through suffering. In what ways has endurance helped you through suffering?

- --endurance is spiritual and unseen. Do you view endurance in this way?
- --can you identify what role endurance has played in your healing process?
- --put it this way: where would you be without endurance?
- --have you found it helpful to learn from other people who have endured? Whom?

STEPPING STONE—Patience

One way to step into the growth point of endurance is through patience. Do you consider yourself to be a patient person?

- --where did you learn or have you learned the value of patience?
- --the opposite of patience is impatience. What do you know about impatience?

--Carl Jung said, "Hurry is not of the devil. Hurry is the devil."
  Is it true for you?
--why do you think there is so much stress, anxiety, worry, and
  anger today?

Patience allows us the luxury of time to think about our deepest commitments. Can you begin to list some of your commitments? Did patience help you with this list?

--with patience come commitment and perseverance. Are these
  good words?
--do you find words like these used much in our fast-paced culture?
--what would it take to slow down? What is preventing you from
  slowing down?
--when you hear love "endures all things" (I Corinthians 13:7),
  what do you think?

Part Three
Living the Vision

8
Godliness

Make every effort to add to your faith with…godliness
(2 Peter 1:6)

The double helix of grace and knowledge is often subtle, as it transforms and grows in the vision of our spiritual life. Putting faith into practice, putting faith into action, seeing our faith at work, is a physical activity. The spirit changes the body. The spiritual informs the material. The two—body and spirit—are not separate. Body and spirit are working together. The interior and the exterior of life become one. Life in Christ is as real as bread and wine, the hard wood of the Cross, the empty tomb, and yes, even washing the feet of another. *Godliness* is a way of describing our life in Christ. Godliness is at the core of our identities. It is who we are. We are godly people in Christ. Grace and knowledge open our eyes to see this new identity of godliness at work in our spiritual lives as it forms and shapes our character and our mortal lives.

Enter with the disciples into the Upper Room. It is the night before Jesus is crucified. Here the disciples gather, presumably to eat the Passover meal with Jesus. Little do they realize Jesus will be the sacrificial lamb. Little do they think this will be the Last Supper. How are they to know that amongst them is a disciple who will betray Jesus?

Look at the Ethiopian icon that introduces our chapter, and look again at the disciples' eyes. They were taking it all in.

The disciples had gathered with Jesus. Earlier, they had argued among themselves as to who was the greatest (Luke 9:46). It was, in some sense, a silly argument. At the same time, it was somewhat serious, as each disciple wanted to advance in rank and seniority

Then he poured water into a basin and began to wash the disciples' feet and to wipe them with the towel that was tied around him. He came to Simon Peter, who said to him, "Lord, are you going to wash my feet?" Jesus answered, "You do not know now what I am doing, but later you will understand." Peter said to him, "You will never wash my feet." Jesus answered, "Unless I wash you, you have no share with me." Simon Peter said to him, "Lord, not my feet only but also my hands and my head!"
John 13:5-9

and importance. It was apparent that Jesus recognized their "inner thoughts" (Luke 9:47), and as a way to illustrate and use the heat of their argument, he bent down and picked up a child and said, in effect, "Here is the greatest among you—this child!" Identity in Christ, our character in Christ, is found not in who is the greatest but who is the least. Identity in Christ is found not in being a master but in being a servant. Our identity in Christ is first and foremost found in being a child of God.

Jesus reshuffles the way of advancing. It is not necessarily based on merit or accomplishments or results. It has more to do with depending upon and relying upon God's grace and knowing God's love—like a child. There is nothing to prove. No, Jesus is about to make it clear to the disciples that if they want to experience the fullness of life in Christ, it is time to serve. This understanding of service would be for the disciples the example and the way to live in Christ. Listen again to the instruction Jesus gives his disciples: "Whoever wishes to be great among you must be your servant" (Matthew 20:27). The disciples had heard this message of service. Now it was time to serve.

Look at the picture that introduces this chapter. The disciples' eyes say it all. But it is time to move from seeing to believing. It is time for the disciples to claim their identities and their character in Christ. Jesus is out of time here on earth. Now is the time for the disciples to grasp their identities found in the character of godliness so that they too may live forever. On the night before he is betrayed, Jesus brings forth a bowl and prepares to wash the disciples' feet. As he begins to wash their feet, he comes to Peter, who says to Jesus:

> "Lord, are you going to wash my feet?" Jesus answered, "You do not *know* now what I am doing, but later you will understand… Do you *know* what I have done to you…? For I have set for you an example, that you also should do as I have done to you. Very truly, I tell you, servants are not greater than their master, nor are messengers greater than the one who sent them. If you *know* these things, you are blessed if you do them." (John 13:6-17)

The emphasis on *knowing* in the above verses is again a reminder for Peter and for the disciples and for all who seek life in Christ that knowing is not about head knowledge. It is about intimacy with God. When we serve, when we do what Christ has done, when we follow his example, we gain insight and knowledge and our character is formed by godliness. It is here, in this deep understanding of godliness, we claim our identities as "children of God, and if children, then heirs, heirs of God and joint heirs with Christ—if, in fact, we suffer with him so that we also may be glorified with him" (Romans 8:17).

Knowledge and grace were together there in the Upper Room. The disciples knew this night was different. With grace, they would begin to live a different life. This new life was based not on status and recognition but on an identity as a child of God. Grace would help the disciples claim this identity. Grace would help the disciples live a new life in Christ. Grace would wash the disciples' feet and strengthen their bodies for service. It is grace that develops our character in the knowledge of godliness.

Growth Point—Godliness

I can remember as a child, after playing outside all day, being told to wash my hands before dinner. Whenever I would complain, I would hear from the kitchen the saying "cleanliness is next to godliness." I wasn't sure what it meant then, but I wanted to eat, so I washed my hands. Only now, in this later stage of my life, do I recognize the relationship between eating, the ritual of washing of one's hands, and purity and godliness. Washing hands is good hygiene and good manners, to be sure. It is a way of taking care of the body. When it comes to godliness, however, Jesus was more concerned with what was inside the body.

The Pharisees were an easy target of scorn, because they actually thought their external rituals would bring them closer to God regardless of what was going on inside their hearts and minds and souls. It is here, with the Pharisees, we begin to pick up on the phrase "cleanliness is next to godliness." Recall one encounter Jesus had with the scribes and Pharisees where Jesus emphasized that cleanliness was first an inside job:

> Woe to you, scribes and Pharisees, hypocrites! For you clean the outside of the cup and plate, but inside they are full of greed and self-indulgence. You blind Pharisee! First clean the inside of the cup, so that the outside also may become clean. (Matthew 23:25-26)

The Pharisees practiced acts and rituals of purity which kept their appearance clean on the outside, but as Jesus points out, there on the inside, the Pharisees were far from godly. It is not just the Pharisees. Our mortal nature, as a result of sin and our separation from God, is unable to purify our own interior lives. We lack the necessary filter. That is because, for Jesus, purity is first and foremost a matter of the heart. Recall from the beatitudes Jesus saying, "Blessed are the pure in heart, for they will see God" (Matthew 5:8). Again, the question remains, how can I get hold of a pure heart? What does it take to purify my heart?

The answer is, of course, we cannot get hold of pure hearts by our own doing. That is something the Pharisees never quite understood. There is no ritual, no act, and no sacrifice of burnt offerings that will purify our hearts. We are incapable and helpless when it comes to the matter of purifying our own hearts. What is within our capability and what is helpful is turning to God and praying that God will "create in us a clean heart and renew a right spirit within us" (Psalm 51).

One way in which God purifies our hearts is by the simple gift of freedom. In Christ, we are set free. A free heart is similar in many respects to a pure heart. When we are set free, it doesn't mean we are set loose. It means that we have free will and are no longer encumbered by sin or by all the many false idols or addictions that displace God's love. "You were called to freedom, brothers and sisters; only do not use your freedom as an opportunity for self-indulgence, but through love become servants to one another" (Galatians 5:13). Herein, we begin to see how a free heart, a pure heart that is formed and shaped by our life in Christ, directs our will to serve in love.

A free heart is not weighted down by sin. A free heart is not blemished or held in bondage by all the many cravings and ways we have become dependent on this world. A free heart really walks to the beat of its own drum, not because of pride or arrogance but because a heart that has been set free in Christ is a humble heart. A humble heart is a heart that no longer relies on our own self, but it is a heart that relies on a self that is centered in a life in Christ. A humble heart is set free to serve others, and it is pure and sees God at work. A humble heart beats with godliness.

We see godliness in our lives when we are humble. We are humble when we rely on our life in Christ. In Christ, we find freedom. It is a freedom to love God and to love our neighbors as ourselves. And as we rely more and more on God's grace and knowledge of God's work in our lives, our hearts are made clean and a right spirit is set within our character.

This understanding of the relationship between godliness and humility was made clear to the disciples in the Upper Room. They knew the words from the prophet Micah, who asked, "What does the Lord require of you but to do justice, and to love kindness, and to walk humbly with your God?" (Micah 6:8). When Jesus began washing the disciples' feet, the words of the prophet were now embodied right before the disciples' eyes. They had the answer.

Humility and Love

Seeing humility in action from the Lord of life was of course more than Peter could handle. Peter said to Jesus, "You will never wash my feet." Jesus answered Peter, "Unless I wash you, you will have no share with me." Peter then exclaimed, "Lord, not my feet only but also my hands and my head!" (John 13:8-9). In other words, wash my whole body. Wash me through and through. Peter could see the need for change. He saw the importance of what was taking place. His vision for life in Christ was taking on new meaning. Humility was now a core principle.

Have you ever tried to love without being humble? I would say it is impossible. A person who is filled with pride and conceit and self-righteousness and who is full of themselves has no room for love. Yes, love is patient and kind and not envious or boastful or arrogant or rude, as St. Paul writes in his love letter (I Corinthians 13). But if we could paraphrase that letter for a moment, couldn't we say the same thing about humility? Humility is patient and kind, and humility is not envious or boastful, nor is humility arrogant or rude. Humility is like love. A humble person is a loving person. A loving person is humble. Humility opens us to godliness. In fact, humility moves us from being self-centered to now centering our lives on God in Christ, who sets us free to love and to serve.

I saw this radical understanding of humility from a part-time maintenance man on our church staff. He was out of full-time work. His car quit under an expressway. It was past midnight. He was angry. He prayed to God about his desperation. He asked God to show him the way forward. Within seconds, he looked out his windshield and there, under the overpass of the expressway, was a homeless man searching for something to eat from a garbage can. The homeless man pulled out of the garbage a bag with a half-eaten hamburger, and the homeless man began to eat it.

Our maintenance man saw this as a sign from God to feed the hungry. Every Sunday at our coffee hour, he now "sells" day-old cookies given to him by a grocery store, and then he uses the money to buy chicken. With volunteers from the church, he then gives out the chicken and other food items that he has been able to purchase for the hungry. He is known on the street as "the chicken man." His identity has changed. Right before our eyes, he is a new man. He possesses godliness. He has a new heart and a right spirit. He has been set free to serve. He has built a ministry that serves now ten thousand meals a year. Read what a Sunday school child wrote to him:

"Dear Curtis, you are a child of God because you feed people who are less fortunate every Saturday. Thank you for being so caring…"

That note may not seem like much to the eyes of some people, but from my perspective, it is a remarkable expression of love and recognition of godliness one child sees in the action of another. She calls out his identity as a "child of God." It is a godly character formed in humility and made fit for service.

Stepping Stone—Self-Denial

There in the Upper Room, the disciples remembered. How could they forget his words to pick up their crosses and follow him? They remembered his words that if anyone wants to find their life, they must first lose it. Yes, they heard the message of self-denial, and now as he washed their feet, they saw his words put into action. As he broke bread and took the cup, he said, "Do this in remembrance of me." The disciples had an idea of what Jesus meant to give of themselves, to sacrifice, to serve, to humble themselves, and to rely on God. Now, as they left the Upper Room, they would know exactly what Jesus meant. "Do this" means "love like this."

The Kidron Valley is just outside the walls of Jerusalem. As the disciples followed Jesus, there is no record of what was said. Presumably, the walk down through the Kidron Valley was in silence. Again, silence is a form of humility and self-denial. The Kidron Valley is filled with tombstones. It is a burial place. It is the valley of death. Some scholars believe the Kidron Valley is what David referenced in his 23rd Psalm when he wrote, "Yea, though I walk through the valley of death, I shall fear no evil." So they walked through this valley of death under the full Passover moon. There was light still shining in the darkness.

As the disciples followed Jesus up to the Mount of Olives, they saw him go into the Garden of Gethsemane and pray. He had told the disciples to stay awake and watch with him as he prayed. The disciples could not do what Jesus asked. They fell asleep. Perhaps they were tired from the walk, perhaps the emotion and stress of the day was exhausting, maybe it was the wine at the supper; we do not know why they fell asleep. What we do know is they were not physically able, they did not have the strength, they did not have the grace to stay awake.

Gethsemane means "olive press." It is here, in the Garden of Gethsemane, Jesus prays. It is here olives are pressed and the oil is used for everything from making bread to anointing kings to healing the sick. It is here Jesus is pressed, and his oil will be used for our salvation. As Jesus returns to the sleeping disciples, he is surrounded by soldiers and Judas, who has told for a few coins where Jesus can be found. Peter jumps one of the soldiers and actually cuts off the soldier's ear. Jesus immediately reprimands Peter and tells him to put his sword back, and then with a touch of his hand, he heals the soldier's ear. Again, we receive a quick lesson there in the Garden that this is a time to rely on God. This is the time to allow God's grace to work. Now all attention is on God, whose attribute and character of godliness is found first in self-denial. This understanding of self-denial will lead Jesus to the Cross.

Standing outside the praetorium where Pontius Pilate interrogated Jesus, Peter could hear the question asked: "What is truth?" Pilate didn't know. Peter didn't know. Soon Jesus would show once and for all truth. Truth is the Resurrection. Jesus knew this truth. Sometimes, we lack both the knowledge and the grace to understand.

As Peter watched a beaten and battered and disfigured Jesus carry the Cross to Golgotha, the place of the skull, he could take it no more. Peter would go fishing.

Rev. Robert T. Jennings

For Reflection and Discussion

GROWTH POINT—Godliness

Godliness begins with the transformation of character. Are you aware of a different character since you found faith in Christ? Have you added godliness to your faith?

- --why would Jesus point to a child as an example of living in the Kingdom?
- --what is it about a servant that displays Kingdom living?
- --how come the Pharisees missed the point about what makes for godly living?
- --have you thought about having a pure heart and what that means for you?

Take a moment and look again at the Ethiopian icon at the front of this chapter. Why is there such emphasis on their eyes? How would you describe their look and why?

- --when we see godliness in action, what do we look for?
- --in what ways is Jesus demonstrating what godliness looks like to Peter?
- --what do you make of the relationship between humility and love?
- --has your faith brought you to a place where you can add humility to your life?

STEPPING STONE—Self-denial

As you reflect on living a life of godliness, how does self-denial become an important characteristic for your faith? What is the connection of the Cross to self-denial?

- --is self-denial a positive word for you now or do you still consider it negative?
- --what happens when you set self-denial within the context of humility?
- --like the Sunday school child, whom do you know who reflects a godly character?
- --do they also demonstrate a life of and character of self-denial?

May You Live in Christ!

When Jesus washed the disciples' feet, he was practicing humility and self-denial. He also was living a life of godliness by his service. Does your faith motivate you to serve?

- --when Jesus took the bread and cup, he said, "Do this." What did he mean?
- --as the disciples walked through the Kidron Valley, what were they thinking?
- --have you thought of oil and Gethsemane (the oil press) as a place of godliness?
- --if you had been with Peter in the Garden, what might your conversation have been like?

9
Mutual Affection

"Make every effort to add to your faith…mutual affection"
(2 Peter 1:7)

Peter left Jerusalem and walked back to Tiberius. It was here he would look for his boat and go fishing. It was here he would do what he knew best. Here he would rely on his own strength and his own character. Here he would try to go back to the way things were. He would go back home.

Peter had seen what was in the empty tomb. In one sense, he had seen nothing but rolled-up linens. In a far deeper sense, however, he now saw into the kingdom of God. The Law and the Prophets and everything Jesus had said and done were now fulfilled. By looking into the emptiness of the tomb, Peter also had seen the fullness of life. God is with us. Nothing can separate us from the firm grasp of this reality. Even through the power of death, God's power will not let go. All of this became evident to Peter through the resurrection of Jesus. Peter left the empty tomb and began to look for Jesus.

Jesus had appeared to Mary Magdalene. Mary saw Jesus. At first she thought he was the gardener. The closer she came to him, the more she saw. Mary saw that heaven was all about her.

Jesus also was seen by Clopas and his wife, also named Mary, on the way to Emmaus. They discussed life with God, beginning with Moses and the prophets. Their eyes were opened, and when they broke bread with Jesus, their hearts burned with the truth of the Resurrection. Jesus was alive, and Clopas and Mary were alive like never before. Mary had been there at the foot of the Cross, and she

When they had finished breakfast, Jesus said to Simon Peter, "Simon son of John, do you love me more than these?" He said to him, "Yes, Lord; you know that I love you." Jesus said to him, "Feed my lambs." A second time he said to him, "Simon son of John, do you love me?" He said to him, "Yes, Lord; you know that I love you." Jesus said to him, "Tend my sheep." He said to him the third time, "Simon son of John, do you love me?" Peter felt hurt because he said to him the third time, "Do you love me?" And he said to him, "Lord, you know everything; you know that I love you." Jesus said to him, "Feed my sheep."

John 21:15-17

knew who had killed Jesus. She also knew only God could raise Jesus from the dead and only God could bring life. As they walked with Jesus on the road to Emmaus, Mary and Clopas became aware that they were alive to God.

Peter made his way back to Tiberius with a few of the other followers of Jesus. The brothers had dispersed after the Crucifixion. The last three years could have been described as one long fishing trip. During this time with Jesus, Peter's human nature had given way to a spiritual nature, so that he knew in his mind and heart and soul there was so much more going on than he could understand. Over the past three years, Jesus had promised life. He had promised the fullness of life, an abundant life, a life with God, life in the kingdom of God. Yes, Peter had recoiled when thinking about death on the Cross. Most would have recoiled at such a gruesome ending. But perhaps life really had not ended for Jesus.

Peter and a few of the disciples got into the boat and went fishing. No doubt the boat was a reminder of the time Peter and Andrew had gone fishing and Jesus had called them to follow him. Peter had told Jesus to "depart from him," and now Peter realized how foolish that had been. Peter was a sinful man, to be sure, but Jesus had called Peter to follow him to show that there is more to life than sin. Sin had kept so many people away from God, but Jesus was showing them how to get over sin and to live with God. Jesus encouraged Peter to fish for men.

"That night, they caught nothing" (John 21:3). For a fisherman like Peter, that was like adding insult to injury. "Just after daybreak," as the story goes. Daybreak—that means night is over. Daybreak means the light is starting to shine through.

> Just after daybreak, Jesus stood on the beach; but the disciples did not know that it was Jesus. Jesus said to them, "Children, you have no fish, have you?" They answered him, "No." He said to them, "Cast the net to the right side of the boat, and you will find some." So they cast it, and now they were not able to haul it in because there were so many fish. (John 21:4-6)

Tabgha, Israel

The statue of Peter and Jesus at the front of this chapter is located on the banks of the Sea of Galilee. It is there, in Tabgha, that Jesus preached the Sermon on the Mount. It is there as well Jesus took a few barley loaves and some small fish from a boy and performed the miracle of the feeding of the five thousand. This is a sacred place, a holy space. The morning Peter and the disciples saw the resurrected Jesus on the beach, they were just off the shore of this holy ground. Before they could see Jesus, they heard him. When Jesus called to the disciples to cast their nets on the other side of the boat, they did what he told them. It was grace that gave them the strength to do what they would not have been able to do normally on their own. With grace they cast their nets and they pulled up a wide variety of fish. And with grace they knew the voice on the shore was that of the Lord. With grace Peter dove from the boat and with grace he swam to shore.

Exactly what was going through Peter's mind, much less his heart, at this point is not recorded. Once again, his body was doing the talking. Peter swam to the bank and went up on the shore, where breakfast—a meal—was prepared. As bread was broken, Jesus said to Peter three times, "Simon Peter, do you love me?" Three times, Peter replied, "Yes, Lord, you know I love you" (John 21:17). Some scholars look at this repetition of Jesus asking Peter three times as a way of balancing out the three denials Peter made when asked if he were a disciple of Jesus prior to the Crucifixion.

Another insight comes when examining the word *love* in the Greek. It is here the Gospel of John uses two Greek words for love: one is *agape* love and the other is *philia* love. The difference between the two loves is important. Agape love we will discuss in our final chapter, and it is the most extreme form of love that was used in the Christian community as a sacrificial form of love. It is from agape we discover the meaning for our sacramental way of life or a sacred way of life.

Philia love has more to do with brotherly love. It is, in fact, where the name of the city Philadelphia is derived as the city of brotherly love. Philia love is mutual affection, it is care and concern for another's wellbeing. The third time Jesus says to Peter "Do you love (philia) me?" Jesus speaks with this accent on mutual affection. Again, as we look at the statue that introduces our chapter, it is apparent that Jesus stands above Peter. Jesus is the Lord of life. He is also making available to Peter now the kingdom of God. It is as if Peter is being welcomed into the Kingdom. Remember, it was Peter to whom he had given the keys to heaven (Matthew 16:19). Now, as the risen Lord stands over Peter, the vision becomes clear that heaven and life in Jesus can be found here on earth, and Peter recalls the words of Jesus that "whenever two or three are gathered together in my name, I am there in the midst of them" (Matthew 18:20). The veil that has separated heaven and earth has been pulled back by Jesus, and Peter is now getting a glimpse into the Kingdom. It is a moment much like that of the Transfiguration.

What Jesus clearly witnesses for Peter and embodies for Peter is the reality of the resurrected life. The Resurrection means that life with God is greater than life without God, because life with God is now greater than death. Right before Peter's eyes, he sees that in Jesus there is life forever. Life in the Resurrection of Jesus is available here on earth. In the statue at Tabgha, it is as if Jesus is signaling to Peter once again to follow. Once again, Jesus reveals to Peter the glory—the presence of God—that surrounds life in Jesus.

Jesus now says to Peter on the same shore of Tabgha where he delivered the Sermon on the Mount and fed the five thousand, "Feed my sheep." The vision has never been clearer for Peter. Self-denial, picking up and bearing our own crosses, and following the risen Lord are the way and the truth and the life. Giving up our own lives does not mean we are reduced to nothing. It means that we are being made into God's image, where we now have everything. Participation in the divine life of Jesus Christ is available to us—right now—as we feed others in mutual affection.

Growth Point—Mutual Affection

How easy it would have been for the disciples to seek revenge following the Crucifixion. There is no evidence, however, in scripture or in any historical record for that matter, that the disciples plotted or planned any act of retaliation. It does not appear as if they were filled with anger. Rather, there is a sense of joy and peace and kindness that runs through the Book of Acts, which describes the early church.

One of the growth points that Peter identifies in his letter that serves as our framework is "mutual affection." Mutual affection is philia love, and it is a way of participating in the divine life of Jesus Christ. Mutual affection has to do with care. The connection for Peter was made standing there on the shore of the Sea of Galilee in the same spot where Jesus had fed five thousand. Now, the risen Lord turns to Peter and says, in effect, "You feed my sheep." Feed them not only with food, but feed them with food that will last forever. Feed them with affection. Feed them with the bread of life. Show the people that you care for them in my name. To care means to respect and to be present and to help another. It doesn't mean that we are there to "fix" another person or to change another person. We are not God, but we are participating in the divine life through mutual affection. Mutual affection is fulfilling.

Pastor Jack

I recall, about ten years ago, traveling with one of my sons and the youth from our parish on a mission to the Dominican Republic. We were all overwhelmed by the oppressive heat. What was also overwhelming was the oppressive poverty. Our mission was outside of Barahona, and we were back in a Haitian refugee camp. Some of the sights and sounds and smells were difficult for us, and it was depressing. We met every evening and prayed and discussed and unpacked our experiences and provided support one to another. What became apparent to us, however, was the support and the encouragement and the overwhelming joy that we began to receive from the Haitians. They were delightful and they lifted our spirits. We had dentists from our team who were using pliers to pull out teeth that were rotten from sucking on the sugar cane. That was the only equipment we had, but the refugees were so very grateful for the little attention we could give.

The same held true with a makeshift women's clinic we held behind a tent, with a flashlight. It was so very primitive and the medicines we had brought were limited, but again and again we heard the word *gracias*. One mother's child was dying, and we took the child in our arms into town and had the baby's lungs sucked clean at a small clinic. We paid cash for the service and the mother wept for joy.

During the days, many of us worked on building a concrete block "church." It was really a small, one-room structure, so it went up quickly. We took pride in the progress that was made on a daily basis, and the time seemed to fly by, working under the hot sun. We knew that this church would be the only solid structure in the refugee camp, and when hurricanes came in the fall, it would be a place of refuge. There was also a desire on the part of the leaders in the camp to use the structure as a classroom for the children during the day and as a medical center at night. Our work was appreciated, and there was mutual affection between the Haitian refugees and our mission group.

The one thing we held in common was we were all Christian. There was a bond of mutual affection as we sang and prayed and learned from one another. At the conclusion of our stay, we stood in a circle and had Communion around a large stake, which you can see in the picture. We had hung our water bottles and t-shirts on the stake during the week. It was in the center of where all the work had taken place.

The man in the picture with his arm raised is Pastor Jack. I will never forget him. He spoke English with a thick accent during the sermon, and we hung on each word. He expressed his gratitude and his joy, and he was so impressed by the maturity of our group and the spirit that was present among us. He went on to say that the only church in the area had been inhabited by leaders from a Voodoo tribe. Ten years before we had arrived, Pastor Jack had put a stake in the ground which literally staked his claim to the little spot where we all stood. He told us that every morning before the sun rose, he would come to this stake and pray that someday a Christian church would be built on this ground. You can see him holding the stake in the picture.

Pastor Jack closed his comments by saying, "I knew you would come." He added, "I knew God was going to be faithful." I knew we were standing on holy ground and Pastor Jack was a holy man. I learned from him so much. To think Pastor Jack prayed for ten years, and so often I have trouble praying for ten minutes. As I write, I am profoundly aware of the mutual affection we have for one another. A picture of Pastor Jack remains on my desk today, and it is a reminder of "when two or three are gathered together in my name, I will be there in your midst."

Stepping Stone—Worship

Mutual affection with Christ is a way we can participate in the divine life and can join two or three in the truth of the Resurrection. Two people can demonstrate mutual affection. But, as you know, even then it can break down under the weight of our human nature. What Peter learned there on the shore of the Sea of Galilee is that mutual affection is made possible in our spiritual nature through our life in the risen Lord. In other words, a third dimension is required in order for mutual affection to overcome sin and brokenness and the works of the flesh. Such a dimension is revealed to us in the breaking of the bread.

During Communion, we encounter the risen Lord, and he leads us into mutual affection. Mutual affection in worship means that our affection is mutual between heaven and earth, between God and man, through the Spirit and the flesh, and our affection is brought into a divine relationship. This relationship goes back to the original covenant with Noah and with Abraham and Isaac and Jacob. It is a covenant that is sealed by the life of Jesus, who comes to us in our encounter with him in the breaking of the bread.

I know for years I thought the priest, when celebrating the Eucharist at the altar, was a representative figure of Christ. Over the years of ministry, I have been brought to the realization that on many Sundays I am anything but Christ-like in my thoughts and feelings and spirit. I am more closely aligned with Peter. Standing at the altar, I am well aware of my foibles, but I am also aware of my meeting Jesus on the sacred ground of Tabgha and hearing the words "Robin, do you love me?" Every Sunday, I am given the opportunity to say with Peter, "Yes, Lord, you know I love you." And to this affirmation of faith in the risen Lord, the words are then spoken clearly and unequivocally, "Feed my sheep."

That is worship. That is communion. That is the Lord's day. It is a wonderful opportunity and privilege to enter into union with the Lord as we extend mutual affection through the faith community and extend the miracle of the feeding of the five thousand in the celebration of worship. As a body of faith, it is quite literally a corporate experience, as the body of Christ is then brought into the believers' lives as we may "evermore dwell in him and he in us" (*Book of Common Prayer,* p. 337).

Where else can you find a community that is built on mutual affection one for another? Yes, I know all about church squabbles, but as with any family there will be conflict. But our affection for each other and our community gives us the capacity to deal with conflict. It also reveals the person in need of attention and provides the opportunity to care and reach out to each other. The church community is aware of pride and hypocrisy and weakness that run through us, but as we come to the altar on Sundays—like Peter—we fall on our knees and look with awe and wonder at the risen Lord who is in our midst.

Joy comes at those times. We feel joy because we are living and trusting in God. The risen Lord gives us the vision to not only see the kingdom of God but to receive and enjoy life with God, right now.

For Reflection and Discussion

Growth Point—Mutual Affection

Mutual affection offers us a way to participate in the divine nature of Jesus Christ. It does not mean we are to fix another person. It does mean we are to care for them.

--what was going through Peter's mind as he swam to greet the risen Lord?
--in what way did Jesus express "mutual affection" towards Peter?
--why does Tabgha, Israel, represent such a sacred spot for Peter?
--how does the Resurrection of Jesus breathe life into mutual affection?

There on the shore of the Sea of Galilee, Peter is being welcomed into the kingdom of God by the risen Lord. The first words are "Feed my sheep."

--in what ways might we "feed" others? Physically, emotionally, spiritually?
--how will they know we are Christians? By our love?
--what if we don't care? What is the opposite of care? Apathy?
--why is apathy a danger, and how does mutual affection counteract apathy?

GROWTH POINT—Worship

The story of Pastor Jack reminds us of mutual affection and the importance of sacred space. Respond to Pastor Jack's statement: "I knew God was going to be faithful."

--in what ways is worship an expression of mutual affection?
--can you be specific? The music, the prayers, the fellowship, the space? What?
--is Holy Communion for you a way of being fed? In what ways?
--describe how it helps you encounter the risen Lord. Is it like Tabgha?

May You Live in Christ!

    Where else can you find a community that is built on mutual affection one for another? Have you thought of church and worship in this way before?
    --are there other areas of your life that offer mutual affection like worship?
      --how does mutual affection make worship more than just
        an individual act?
      --what do the body of Christ and the bread of heaven signify for you?
      --as you join Peter in worship of the risen Lord, is there joy for you?

10
Love

"Make every effort to add to your faith with…love"
(2 Peter 1:7)

We come not to the end of our study but now really the beginning. Peter calls upon us to add to our faith "love." This is, of course, agape love. It is sacrificial love. It is the kind of love that makes life sacred. So much of our understanding of love today is based on delight. It is like banana pudding. I would "love" to eat that banana pudding, we think to ourselves. Is that really love? Is love simply about devouring and consuming? Is love just a one-way relationship? In other words, how do you think the poor banana pudding feels? Is love just about ourselves, our needs, our gratification, our desires?

So many people have become so disillusioned by this word—*love*. Yes, books and libraries have been filled trying to explain love. Some of us are old enough to remember the movie *Bob & Carol & Ted & Alice*, about "wife swapping," as it was called in the 1960s. If you don't know the movie, it is not worth seeing. I bring it up only because of the theme song: "What the world needs now is love, sweet love." That really is not the kind of love our world needs now. *Eros* love is erotic love, and it is a far cry from agape love, which is sacrificial love.

When Jesus bids us to "follow him," it is into a life of self-denial. In our day and age, such a life of self-denial sounds so countercultural. Well, it is. But by denying ourselves, we find that once we get ourselves out of the way we are able to really respond to the other in love and to allow God to enter in ways that are far beyond our imagination. We discover that faith and love complement one another. Faith and love work together in a way that is truly remarkable. Recall in scripture we are

"Very truly, I tell you, when you were younger, you used to fasten your own belt and to go wherever you wished. But when you grow old, you will stretch out your hands, and someone else will fasten a belt around you and take you where you do not wish to go." (He said this to indicate the kind of death by which he would glorify God.) After this he said to him, "Follow me."

John 21:18-20

taught: "God is love, and those who abide in love abide in God, and God abides in them" (I John 4:16). How do we abide in God? Faith. How do we abide in love? Faith.

With faith, then, comes God. "God is love," John claims, and then he goes on to further this powerful insight by writing "There is no fear in love, but perfect love casts out fear" (I John 4:18). Again, we might wonder what makes love perfect. Obviously, God makes love perfect. Furthermore, our faith in God perfects or completes love. Once again, this little Bible verse is a big reminder of the importance found in faith and love working together. Love is about faith and God. Love is not necessarily about feeling good or having our needs met or about our being nice and sweet. But with love and faith, we now have the capability to cast out fear and give of ourselves.

Love, then, is simply and quite profoundly the will to extend ourselves for the good of another. Remember, *good* is derived from *God*. So when we extend ourselves for the good of another, we are really opening a way for God to be at work in another through love. It is a beautiful understanding of life and faith and love. And it works.

Growth Point—Love

We see this picture of love in the life of St. Peter most graphically depicted in the introduction of our chapter painted by the artist Caravaggio. As is typical with Caravaggio's works, one immediately is struck by the contrast of light and dark. The background in the painting is not important for Caravaggio. What is important and what the artist wants the viewer to see are the characters and the action that is taking place. Caravaggio demands our attention and focuses our eyes as if he is shining a light on the subject. And the subject is complex. It is, in one sense, a picture of brutality and three men tying and binding another man to a cross as they prepare to kill him. We are looking at the face of death. But having now studied the spiritual growth of St. Peter, we realize that he is losing his life in order to find it. We are aware that he is fulfilling the words of the risen Lord, who said to Peter there on the shores of the Sea of Galilee, "'you will be taken where you do not wish to go.' Jesus said this to indicate the kind of death by which Peter would glorify God" (John 21:18).

This sounds horrific to modern ears. However, having had a son in the military, I am always struck when I hear the words in the Gospel: "No one has greater love than this, to lay down his life for his friends." We were struck as a nation by this understanding of sacrifice following the terrorist attack on our country during 9/11 and the sacrifice of the police and firefighters. In the aftermath of school shootings, we are all sensitive to the teachers who stand in harm's way in safeguarding and protecting their children. The list goes on and on about this heroic, sacrificial form of love. It is the ultimate form of sacrifice.

It is in this spirit we gaze at the picture before us. Death is not idealized. The executioners are nothing but thugs. They are doing their job. They are performing a task. The viewer can see how they are straining and how they enter our space with the rump of one who is using his back as he struggles to lift the cross. Peter is being hoisted upside down as he is crucified, because he considers himself unworthy to die in the same way as Jesus. It is difficult to see what Peter is focusing on—if anything at all. Is he looking at the nail in his hand and wondering if it will hold him? Is he looking at the ground or the hole where the cross is going and wondering if his head will be crushed? Perhaps he is looking at spectators or loved ones who are witnessing these final moments of his life. The artist intentionally leaves us guessing. What is clear and what is perfectly within our grasp of knowledge is that the executioners are not taking Peter's life. No, no, no…a hundred times over, no. No one is taking Peter's life. He is giving his mortal life. His spiritual growth has led him to the place where he knows there is a greater life. His life with God—who is the source of love—will take over through faith at this point of the crucifixion. The crucifixion is what St. Paul refers to as a "momentary affliction that is preparing us for an eternal weight of glory beyond all measure, for we look not at what can be seen but at what cannot be seen; for what can be seen is temporary, but what cannot be seen is eternal" (II Corinthians 4:18).

Perhaps, from our perspective, we might now see Peter focused on the vision of God's kingdom that is opening right before his eyes. Love has a way of opening our eyes to see God. Perfect love especially has a way of helping us see God at work in our lives, because perfect love combines love with faith. Perfect love—don't forget—also casts out all fear. In this painting by Caravaggio, we see the depiction again of the irony that it is the executioners who are straining and literally bent out of shape. The sacrificial love that Peter demonstrates has no fear. It is this love that is built upon a rock. It is love that "bears all things, believes all things, hopes all things, and endures all things. Love never ends" (I Corinthians 13:7-8).

Love Leads

Following the resurrection of Jesus and Peter's encounter with the risen Lord on the shore of the Sea of Galilee, it became apparent to Peter that Jesus, through the power of the Resurrection, had broken down the walls that separated heaven from earth, man from God, and the limits of time and space to a far deeper understanding of the timeless nature of God who permeates all space and all matter. At the heart of God and at the center of God's cosmos is love. Peter left the shores of the Sea of Galilee and, without any of the modern forms of today's technology, communicated with the disbanded group of disciples and gradually began to bring them back together. Rather than plotting and planning how to retaliate and how to vent their anger over the Crucifixion of Jesus, they began to focus their vision on the Resurrection.

In the book of Acts, we read more about the life of Peter and the disciples following the Resurrection of Jesus. It is apparent that their spiritual life came alive and grew and matured with the gift of the Holy Spirit on the day of Pentecost. It is the Holy Spirit who reveals Christ in our lives. It is the Holy Spirit who unites and relates us to the will of God. It is the Holy Spirit who was actively involved in the lives of the disciples as they followed the risen Lord in all that they said and did. It was through the power of the Holy Spirit the church was formed by the revelation of Jesus, and it is through the power of the Holy Spirit the church is now still shaped by being united one with another through the body of Christ in the breaking of the bread and related to one another in doing God's will.

"Will you restore the Kingdom to Israel?" the disciples asked Jesus before he ascended to heaven and was crowned as Lord over both heaven and earth (Acts 1:6). To this, Jesus replies, "You will receive power when the Holy Spirit has come upon you; and you will be my witnesses" (Acts 1:8).

It is again the Holy Spirit who reveals Kingdom life. We might ask, "What does this Kingdom life look like?" In a word, it looks like love. It looks like acceptance and mercy and forgiveness and also joy and peace and hope, and all those words that come flowing out of our spiritual life are now seen in the Kingdom life. Peter clearly, through the power of the Holy Spirit, now has one foot in the Kingdom. The more he sees of the Kingdom, the more he bears witness to life in the Kingdom here on earth. Story after story, chapter after chapter, the book of Acts tells of the power the disciples received as a result of the Holy Spirit. It was through the Holy Spirit the disciples became the witnesses Jesus called them to be, by living and relying on the life in the kingdom of God. The disciples were empowered to witness and lead others to this life that really is life. It is life in Christ who is Lord of life. Hear Peter as he writes in his first letter to the early church: "Above all, maintain constant love for one another, for love covers a multitude of sins" (1 Peter 4:8). Clearly, Peter has become a witness for Christ and the church and one who is now known for leading in love. Peter has changed. Peter has spiritually grown through the vision of his life in Christ.

Love Never Ends

As the church of Jesus Christ was growing in numbers, Peter and the other disciples traveled out of Jerusalem bearing witness to the risen Lord. In obedience to Jesus, they preached a gospel of the agape love they had experienced on the Cross and the same love in Christ who stepped out of the empty tomb on that first Easter morning. Jesus lives! There was no past tense when preaching about Jesus. Jesus is in the present tense and future tense. And because Jesus lives, we too now have life in him. *Vivatis in Christo!* May you live in Christ!

Through the power of the Holy Spirit, Peter proclaimed this gospel, this good news, "to the uttermost ends of the earth" (Acts 1:8). Exactly where he went is hard to calculate, but it appears that over the years he travelled from Babylon to Antioch and to Greece. Legend also has Peter making journeys as far as the British Isles, where Westminster Abbey is technically named for him, and in France he was the patron saint of the cathedral in Chartres. Peter ended his travels in Rome upon completing what Jesus had commanded him to do.

Peter was not alone in his evangelical zeal. In Rome, Peter was accompanied no doubt by Paul, who helped him to develop the churches and early Christian gatherings in the first century. The fact that Peter worshipped with early Christians is assumed, as worship was central to the Christian practice. The fact that worship was probably hidden or underground and removed from most Romans is also understood. The fact that there is little written about the Christian movement during the period of Nero's persecutions is understandable, because why on earth would you want to draw unnecessary attention to yourself with someone like Nero? The fact that the early Christian movement grew was a result of their undying love and belief that life is found in the resurrected Christ.

We also know that crazed emperor Nero blamed the Christians for the devastating fire that spread throughout much of Rome. There were already early records and historical documents that referred to Christian persecutions, but with Nero, the atrocities amounted to a full-scale slaughter. There were crucifixions and tortures that reflected a barbaric and savage Roman emperor. Few citizens complained over these atrocities, because to do so would have resulted in certain death. With Nero seeking revenge for the fire and a possible political shield, many scholars believe that it was during this period Nero had both Peter and Paul arrested and jailed as political scapegoats for the fire.

Whether or not Peter and Paul were in prison at the same time is again up for debate. What does seem highly probable is that the main prison during this time of Nero's persecutions (approximately 67 AD) was the dreaded Mamertine Prison. No doubt both Peter and Paul were in this prison. Visitors to Rome can still see this dreaded chamber of horror. The prison is designed with two levels, with one on top of the other. The top level of the prison has some light entering and a reasonable height to move around. That is not to speak well of it, except that compared to the lower prison, it didn't have the indignity and disgust of human waste being shoveled down from above. To say the dark, smelly lower level was a snake pit is a mild understatement. It was here prisoners were thrown down in the damp and cold to die. If the torture and cruelty of the guards didn't kill you, the disease and the frigid temperatures of Roman winters would take away whatever breath was left in you. In this prison, Peter was reported to have been thrown into this lower level, but he still witnessed and converted fellow prisoners and a few jailers. Most in this prison only sought death, but Peter again sought souls for whom life in Christ could be experienced, even in their weary and dank surroundings.

Tradition has it that Paul was beheaded and Peter was crucified. What is unusual is that often, in the case of rabble rousers, their bodies would be burned after their deaths, so that little of their remains could be recovered by any followers. The underground catacombs in Rome are in fact filled with burial sites for those early Christians who died of natural causes, but with Peter, the belief was his body was removed after his crucifixion by faithful Christians. Rather than place him in a catacomb where his body could be apprehended by the Romans, believers in the early church hid his body under the secret altar where they worshipped. Eventually, when only the skeleton remains from Peter were left, they gathered the bones and placed them in an ossuary. It is in this box, scholars believe, they found the bones of St. Peter, and they were formally identified by Pope Paul VI on June 26, 1968.

Stepping stone—Participants of the Divine Nature

Agape love is a distinctive Christian form of love that is not simply based on our deeds or our actions but first and foremost on God's love. In our study of St. Peter, in chapter after chapter, we learned of his humanity as a result of his human foibles. We also learned that St. Peter grew in his spiritual formation around his life in Christ. It was the spiritual nature of Peter that was aware of God's love always being extended to him. Whether he was in a boat fishing with Andrew or climbing high up on the Mount of Transfiguration, Peter was seeing God's love at work in his life. By participating in this "divine nature," or this love of God, Peter realized he was loved by God more and more.

> We love because God first loved us. Those who say "I love God" and hate their brothers and sisters are liars; for those who do not love a brother or sister whom they have seen cannot love God, whom they have not seen. The commandment we have from him is this: those who love God must love their brothers and sisters also.
>
> (I John 4:19-21)

This understanding of love demonstrates that God is the source of love. We are in danger when we think for a minute that somehow we are the source of love. No, God's love works in and through us. We can, however, participate in the divine nature of God's love by training and disciplining our lives. The idea of developing a discipline or being disciplined sounds unappealing to many in our compulsive, addictive culture. It is in the disciplined life around the life of Christ we find our spirits formed and our character shaped and closely aligned with the disciples. The word *discipline*, as you can tell, is not far removed from the word *disciple*.

To be a disciple means that we are disciplined because we have a teacher, an instructor, a guide, a person who will actually lead us. That person is, of course, Jesus Christ. He is someone we can believe in, and Jesus is the same "yesterday, today, and forever" (Hebrews 13:8).

Like Peter, we are being called to now follow Jesus. Follow him into an abundant life. Follow him into a life with God. Follow him into an eternal life that never ends. As we follow him, we will participate in his life, and he will participate in ours. As we act in his life, so he will act in our lives. As we become more involved and take part in the life of Christ, so his life will become more involved and take part in ours. It is here, in our participation in the divine nature of Jesus Christ, we experience a blessing. It is a blessing for life. It is a blessing that casts a vision for life. Look now as "eyewitnesses of his majesty" (2 Peter 1:16) to Peter, who leaves us with his final blessing.

Rev. Robert T. Jennings

For Reflection and Discussion

GROWTH POINT—Love
Perfect love has a way of helping us see God at work, because perfect love combines love with faith. Have you ever thought of love as perfect? Is it a fantasy?
   --scripture tells us that "God is love" (I John 4:16). Is that perfect?
   --in what ways has your faith helped you grow to see this love of God?
   --why does scripture tells us that "perfect love casts out fear" (I John 4:18)?
   --is that true for Peter? Is that true for you?

Love is simply the will to extend ourselves for the good of another. Does that help you think about agape love in a way that can encourage you to give of yourself?
   --where have you learned about love? What do you know about agape love?
   --have you thought of love as sacrificial? Is that what makes love sacred?
   --in what ways does love seem eternal or "never ending" (I Corinthians 13:8)?
   --how does the resurrection of Jesus open our eyes to see the kingdom of God?

STEPPING STONE—*Participants of the Divine Nature*
God's love works in and through us. We can participate in the divine nature of God's love by training and disciplining our lives. Why is this training important?
   --Peter tells us to escape lust and become participants of the divine nature. Why?
   --in what ways does agape love help you escape the "corruption" Peter refers to?
   --do you see yourself or have a vision for participating in the divine nature?
   --what might that look like? Have the growth points Peter identifies helped?

May You Live in Christ!

Jesus now calls us to follow him. Follow him into an abundant life. Follow him into a life with God. Follow him into an eternal life that never ends. How does that sound?

    --do you think of your life as never ending? Do you think of never dying?
    --what might life eternal be like? Is that something we can experience now?
    --have you placed your confidence and trust in Jesus Christ?
    --has that helped you to see your life as a participation in his divine nature?

11
Benediction

*Grow in the grace and knowledge of our
Lord and Savior Jesus Christ
(2 Peter 3:18)*

The benediction comes at the end of the service, and although this is not a worship service but a book, I am still a clergyman. I like benedictions and it seems fitting to have one at the end of this book. What better person than St. Peter to leave us with his benediction? The word *benediction* is derived from the Latin words *bene* and *dictum,* which together mean literally "a good word." The good word St. Peter leaves with us is "grow." Throughout our study, we have been examining spiritual growth. Spiritual growth is possible. Spiritual growth can be measured. There are ways to spiritually grow, and St. Peter has provided us with a vision for growth through the power of the Holy Spirit.

The movements within the Holy Spirit are subtle and such change is often not seen, but it occurs when we receive the vision of God at work through everything in our lives. When we see God's glory, we begin to receive this vision of God as light who enlightens us with his presence in our lives. Yes, when we receive the vision of faith, we are able to grow in leaps and bounds by recognizing hope and peace and love and joy in our everyday experiences.

Our spiritual growth with St. Peter continues as we add to our faith by seeing God in such areas of our life as goodness, knowledge, self-control, and endurance. So often, when people talk in spiritual terms, it can sound like fluff. But as Peter tells us, we see the vision of the risen Lord come alive as a reality when we grow and our character is shaped and formed into a life of godliness, mutual affection, and love.

May You Live in Christ!

And I tell you, you are Peter, and on this rock I will build my church, and the gates of Hades will not prevail against it. I will give you the keys of the kingdom of heaven, and whatever you bind on earth will be bound in heaven, and whatever you loose on earth will be loosed in heaven.

(Matthew 16:18-19)

Christian spiritual growth comes with the vision that "God so loved the world that he gave his only Son, so that everyone who believes in him may not perish but may have eternal life" (John 3:16). Eternal life, zoe life, abundant life, enters our mortal lives like a seed planted or a cell that grows and expands through the double helix of grace and knowledge.

Grace and knowledge work together. Grace informs our knowledge about God. Knowledge shapes our minds with the grace of God. Together, grace and knowledge open our minds and our hearts and our wills to love God and our neighbor as ourselves. Grace and knowledge help us grow with a vision for the kingdom of God, and by interacting with God through grace and knowledge, we have life with God. This life is a new life, and "this is eternal life, that they may know you, the only true God and Jesus Christ whom you have sent" (John 17:3).

St. Peter grew in this grace and knowledge, and he was given the keys to the kingdom of heaven. And one key that St. Peter holds out to us is the key of spiritual growth. This key is personally designed to fit and unlock our own hearts. It is the key that turns our life in Christ into a blessing—right now.

Vivatis in Christo! May you live in Christ!

Amen.

Image credits

Introduction
The floor plan appears in *The Bones of St. Peter: the First Full Account of the Discovery of the Apostle's Tomb.* John Evangelist Walsh. Sophia Institute Press, 1982.

Chapter 1
The Disciples Peter and John Running to the Sepulcher on the Morning of the Resurrection, c. 1898 (oil on canvas) by Eugène Burnand (1850-1921). Musee d' Orsay, Paris. The Bridgeman Art Library.

Chapter 2
The Transfiguration, c. 1520 (oil on wood) by Raphael (1483-1520). Vatican City. The Bridgeman Art Library

Chapter 3
Christ Walking on Water and Reaching Out His Hand to Save Saint Peter, c. 19th. by Ferdinand Victor Eugene Delacroix (1798-1863). Private collection. The Bridgeman Art Library.

Chapter 4
Jesus Feeds the 5000, c. 1999 by Laura James. Permission granted by the artist.

Chapter 5
The Calling of the Apostles Peter and Andrew, c. 1308-1311 (tempera on wood) by Duccio di Buoninsegna (c. 1255-1260; 1318-1319). National Gallery of Art, Washington, D.C. The Bridgeman Art Library.

Chapter 6
The Denial of Peter, c. 1660 (oil on wood) by Rembrandt Harmensz van Rijn (1606-1669). Rijksmuseum, Amsterdam. The Bridgeman Art Gallery.

Chapter 7

Jesus Healing the Leper, Frank Wesley. Permission granted by Athalie Wesley.

Chapter 8

Jesus Washing Peter's Feet. Ethiopian icon. Picture taken by John Kohan. Permission granted.

Chapter 9

Statue of Peter and Jesus by the Sea of Galilee, at the Church of the Primacy of Peter in Tabgha, Israel. Photo and permission by Robert Quaife.

Chapter 10

Crucifixion of St. Peter, c. 1601 (oil on canvass) by Caravaggio (1571-1610) Cerasi Chapel of Santa Maria del Popolo in Rome. The Bridgeman Art Library.

Chapter 11

The Statue of St. Peter. c. 1838-1840 (marble) sculpted by Giuseppe De Fabris (1790-1860). St. Peter's Basilica, Vatican City. iStockphoto